The Wardrobe of Inner Beauty

A Bible Study for Women

Bonnie Foxley

Waterfall Publishing
Woodinville, WA

ISBN-13: 978-1973810308
ISBN-10: 1973810301

Library of Congress Control Number: 2017913022
CreateSpace Independent Publishing Platform
North Charleston, South Carolina

I dedicate this book to my beautiful Lord and Savior, Jesus Christ. Thank-you for loving me and calling me to serve You. It has been a sweet life of love and I look forward to the future with You as You provide day to day. "He who called you is faithful and He will bring it to pass." (I Thessalonians 5:24)

Acknowledgements

This book has been many years in the making and it would not be anywhere without the encouragement of my sweet husband, Bryan. Thanks for believing in the gift enough to keep reminding me to work on it and for your constant love and support through all our years together. I love you!

Thanks to Nancy Aguilar for the editing help and for your encouragement for me to pull it off the shelf. Your gentle advice and help were from the Lord Himself.

Thanks to my parents, Warren and Ruby Stewart who raised me, by their gracious example, to love our beautiful Lord and to pursue Him with my whole heart. Many thanks for all the help and advice through the years. I miss you, Dad, but look forward to being reunited in His Kingdom soon. Thank-you to my siblings, Priscilla, Paul, Angela and Elise and your families who I love and admire greatly.

Thanks to my kids and their spouses for enduring all my silly ideas and for their love. Thanks to my daughter, Allison for modeling many times and for always 'being game.' Austin and Karen, Collin and Andrew I love you all so much!

Thanks to the many friends, who have been through the study or the fashion show already, for your encouragement; Jeannie, Joanne, Nancy, Cathy, Wendy, Laurie and Leesha to name a few. Thanks to Lori Moloney and Jill Byington for your earlier editing help.

Thanks to Jeffrey McCormack for the cover art and Kai Chinn for author photo.

Thanks to my church, Calvary Fellowship in Seattle, and to Wayne and Cathy Taylor and all the great teachers who have taught me and inspired me to keep serving our Lord.

Table of Contents

Introduction

It's another rushed morning and I'm stuck in front of my bedroom mirror, frantically searching for the right outfit. "Ready, Hon?" I hear my husband calling from downstairs.

"Be right there," I yell. Then I mutter, "That is, if I ever find something to wear!" All I want is an outfit that makes me feel confident, comfortable, and attractive. Really, is that too much to ask?

I think about the day ahead and meeting up with my friend from school days, Kristy, who always looks perfectly cute, trim, and fashionable. Even though we have a good time on the surface, I've always sensed a secret competition going on between us. I want to dress right around her. I don't want to look too old, too young, too stuffy, or too flashy. I grab a hanger and face my reflection, holding up a paisley print top over my nice jeans. *Hmmm, how about this*? I turn sideways for a profile view. *No way—it makes me look fat.* How can I have so many nice clothes and suddenly hate all of them?

My twelve-year-old son calls out next. "Mom I can't be late! Are we leaving soon?"

"Yeah, Sweetie, almost ready," I lie. Minutes later, I settle for the black, loose-fitting sweater that covers my rear end. I throw it on over my head—hoping my dangly earrings and sparkly sandals will distract from my fashion inadequacies—and I fly out the door.

As women, we're hopelessly obsessed with beauty. In 2013, women in the US spent a total of $116.4 billion on apparel alone (https://www.npd.com). Another $54 billion was spent on skin care products, health club memberships, diet foods, and cosmetic surgery. Ladies, we could have bailed out several poor countries with the money spent on fashion! Not only does our unquenchable drive for outward beauty cost money, but it also consumes unquantifiable amounts of our time and energy. Many of us feel emotional distress over our weight and resort to fad diets or eating disorders. In our desperate pursuit of an attractive appearance, do we believe beauty to be nothing more than visual perfection?

We work so hard to pursue a fleeting thing. And when we finally reach our goal of perfection, how long can we hold on to it? Five years? Ten? Let's face it—gravity and time take their toll on even the most attractive women among us.

Our desire to be beautiful is natural. In fact, when pursued in balance, this desire is a healthy part of who we are. Yet unfortunately in our culture, we have a distorted value structure because we're bombarded with images of surgically enhanced bodies and air-brushed complexions. This so-called "ideal" look can destroy our perception of true beauty. You know what I'm talking about—Barbie incarnate! Celebrities are exalted to goddess status, influencing their fans far beyond the silver screen. We follow them on social media, watch them on TV, and read about them in magazines, where they mandate everything from shampoo to software. Our competitive nature responds by comparing ourselves and then wondering why we never measure up. This constant striving often ends in despair.

What do we hope to gain from looking beautiful? Deep down, I believe most of us think beauty will bring us the attention and approval we crave—the universal need of every human heart. Admittedly, our culture favors attractive people with better jobs, paychecks, and promotions. After all, Ken and Barbie seem to have it all. Does that mean the rest of us become second-class citizens when we lose our youthful figure and put on a little too much weight? No! Thankfully God has a completely different value system. Let's go back to that upstairs mirror and ponder a new scenario:

I'm peacefully getting dressed, reflecting on my Bible reading from that morning. As I think about the day ahead and the people I'll see, I begin praying, *Lord, Sue seems a little down lately. Please clothe me with Your compassion today so I can show her Your love. And Lord, I need to perform at work with a better attitude. You know how my supervisor gets on my nerves. Please clothe me with humility toward her. I also need Your garments of patience and kindness so I can be sweet to my kids today. Oh yes, and as I meet up with Judy for lunch, please adorn me with Your necklace of discernment. Help me give Your wise counsel about her troubled marriage.*
Next, I look in the mirror and notice how wide my thighs look. I resist the urge to grab a cookie and jump back into bed. Instead, I pray: *Lord, I know I'm not in the best shape right now. Cover me in Your righteousness because it's You I want people to see in me anyway.* I spray on a little perfume and thank Him for providing a custom-made wardrobe just for me, perfect for every circumstance. What a privilege to have my very own heavenly designer!

A truly beautiful woman glows from the inside out. She exudes confidence and joy that outshine physical appearance. She makes others feel loved and accepted, and serves without thought of recognition. Her inner beauty is an extraordinary sight to behold. She's the lovely and gracious person God created her to be.

The idea for this study came during a dark season in my life, a time when I was often the insecure woman in the opening scene. Physical beauty—and my perceived lack of it—was overly important to me. I felt embarrassed to pray about my obsession because it seemed so unspiritual. I knew the warning from Proverbs 31:30, "Beauty is vain" (KJV). Maybe my insecurities were intensified by my early years working as a model and competing in beauty pageants. At that time, I believed contentment could only be achieved by measuring up to this elusive standard of beauty and achievement.

One scripture passage the Lord gave me during that time was Isaiah 60:1-2, and it's become the key for this study: "Arise, shine; for your light has come! And the glory of the Lord is risen upon you. For behold, the darkness shall cover the earth, and deep darkness the people; but the Lord will arise over you, and His glory will be seen upon you." As I meditated on these words, the Lord began showing me His answer to my problem.

The personal encouragement God provided from His Word was exactly what I needed. Since then, whenever I struggle with the issue of beauty, a fresh understanding of His promises lifts my feelings of inadequacy. His Word gives me hope and changes my thinking to a correct, godly view of myself. Scripture helps me remember my calling—to share the good news of God's love to my world. And I want to share that love with you too.

As we study God's Word, we realize He's provided everything we need to be beautiful in the truest sense. He has an exciting plan for our spiritual adornment, and He wants us to rise up and become radiant with the beauty He gives. It doesn't matter what physical features we're given at birth—God's genuine beauty is for all of us. This beauty goes beyond outward appearance, and it touches lives forever. As we live more in love with our Lord Jesus and wear the clothing (or qualities) He gives, we truly become more beautiful, generous, giving, and multi-talented. We become the women He created us to be.

God's design for our relationship with Him is to live in the center of His incomparable, unconditional love. I Corinthians 13:4-8 describes that love:

"Love suffers long and is kind; love does not envy, love does not parade itself, is not puffed up; does not behave rudely, does not seek its own, is not provoked, thinks no evil; does not rejoice in iniquity, but rejoices with the truth; bears all things, believes all things, hopes all things, endures all things. Love never fails."

In this book, we'll examine the many character qualities of God's incredible love and learn about the new wardrobe He provides. In this wardrobe, complete with cosmetics and accessories, we'll look at pieces like the Garment of Praise, the Garment of Kindness, and the Ring of Relationship.

The glorious wardrobe of God's love is meant for you and me. As Christian women, we have a unique calling to live out the Lord's character to others, and this is the essence of true beauty. May you be encouraged as you read and practice *the Wardrobe of Inner Beauty*.

Chapter One

Arise, Shine!

"Arise, shine; for your light has come! And the glory of the Lord is risen upon you. For behold, the darkness shall cover the earth, and deep darkness the people; but the Lord will arise over you, and His glory will be seen upon you." (Isa. 60:1-2)

We've all watched heads turn when a gorgeous woman enters a room. Exuding confidence and security, this woman commands attention even when she's dressed in blue jeans. We've also probably seen a woman enter a room appearing hunched over and insecure. Though dressed well, her stylish clothes don't necessarily make her attractive. Outgoing Susie in workout pants beats Moody Marge in a designer dress every time. What's the winning attitude we're talking about? Not arrogance but a comfortable confidence. And there's a big difference.

Isaiah 60:1 says it best: "Arise, shine, for your light has come and the glory of the Lord has risen upon you." As Christian women, we've received a priceless gift—a light to shine—and we're commissioned by God to offer it to the world around us. He's charged us to stand up straight, smile, and share His love. It's a command, not an option. Should we wait until we feel "special" before sharing His light? No! Sadly, many things keep us from shining brightly, namely our sin, pain, and fear. All affect our countenance (our ability to shine) and even our posture (our ability to rise).

If you've accepted Christ as your Savior, you are beautiful because Jesus, the glory of God, lives inside you! Galatians 2:20 says, "It is no longer I who live, but Christ lives in me." Our faith makes this truth evident. Because as Jesus forgives our sins, heals our hurts, and works through us, we become a testimony of His glory.

Living in a fallen world, we all carry emotional baggage. Invariably, we pick up the burden of our trials. Some women carry more than their share, experiencing deep pain or abuse. Instead of typical smile lines, their faces may be etched with sadness and bitterness. Perhaps the sparkle of innocence has faded from their eyes, and their posture appears stooped.

Working in prison ministry, I've met many women ruined by sin. They wear the effects on their faces, and it's sad to see their physical beauty has faded. When one vibrant eighteen-year-old became addicted to meth, her appearance deteriorated with each passing year. By age twenty-eight, she looked in her sixties, with sunken eyes, gray complexion, and sores covering her body. Other sins may not seem as obvious, but *all* sin takes a toll on our God-given inner and outer beauty. The Lord never meant for us to carry our burdens this way! Still other women have experienced great emotional and/or physical trauma, yet they radiate joy because Jesus has touched and healed their hearts. He's given them beauty for ashes, as it says in Isaiah 61:3.

Whatever our load may be, we can confidently leave it with the Lord by faith, and keep leaving it there until the burden is lifted. The path to healing isn't always easy—it's a daily, dependent walk with our Savior. Unpacking those heavy suitcases is something He does *with* us. In His mercy, He helps us put things right, one piece at a time.

Hebrews 12:1-2 encourages us to "lay aside every weight, and the sin which so easily ensnares us, and…run with endurance the race that is set before us, looking unto Jesus, the author and finisher of our faith."

The Beauty Robber

The first step toward true beauty is to repent of sin, which is the number-one beauty robber. Confess everything. Tell Jesus whatever is holding you back from fixing your eyes completely on Him. He wants to forgive and deliver you from it. I John 1:9 assures us that "if we confess our sins, He is faithful and just to forgive us our sins and to cleanse us from all unrighteousness."

There are as many sins as human experiences. Maybe you're trapped by anger, self-centeredness, or addiction. Jesus came to save you from the effects of sin—eternal death and hell—and to set you free from sin's grip. Seek Him through His Word, commit it to Him in prayer, and experience His support through fellowship with other believers. It may take time for victory to come, but persevere and have patience. He will do it!

Often, we shift blame for our actions onto others. We say, "He made me do it!" or "I'm so mad I have to swear" or "I'm drunk because my parents were drunks!" The truth is, *we* are in control and we're accountable to God for everything we do, say, and think.

If we're mixed up with the sinful behavior of others, our sin may turn into a tangled mess and truth may be hard to distinguish. There are always two sides to a conflict, and we must take responsibility for our part. If someone has truly wronged us, we may need to repent of the ensuing bitterness and retaliation we desperately want to harbor.

Sin is any action against God's will, and His will is spelled out in the Bible. Jesus simplified God's will for us in the New Testament when He summarized all the commandments in Matthew 22:37-40: "'You shall love the Lord your God with all your heart, with all your soul, and with all your mind.' This is the first and great commandment. And the second is like it: 'You shall love your neighbor as yourself.' On these two commandments, hang all the Law and the Prophets."

When you're trying to decide what to do in a situation, try asking yourself, *Will this decision show love toward God and others?* Let's say you're in the grocery store craving your favorite candy bar, and you're a little short on cash. You think, *I could easily slip this in my purse and no one would even notice. Besides, it only costs a dollar!* The decision to shoplift doesn't show love to God because it's breaking the eighth commandment: "You shall not steal" (Ex. 20:15). Also, shoplifting isn't trusting God to provide your needs. And from the storeowner's perspective, she already has a hard time making her payroll and taxes every month so you wouldn't be showing love by ripping her off.

How about murder? Never! Adultery or sex outside of marriage? It may sound tempting, but no! Committing sexual sin doesn't show love to our spouse, to someone else's spouse, or to any other person we may want to be with.

Less obvious sins creep into our lives as well. Maybe we neglect our household chores for days so we can keep up with social engagements. But love teaches us to take care of the home and family God's given us. Love compels us to provide an organized, healthy, peaceful environment.

Love has priorities. God wants you to love Him first and give Him your heart. If you're married with a family, love your husband next and then your children. After that comes your home and then other ministries and relationships. This order can be difficult to live out because even little compromises may hurt others.

Sin blocks the flow of love, life, and beauty that the Lord desires to share through us. But when we're motivated by God's love, we see the needs of others and are inspired by the Holy Spirit to do good for them. The Christian life becomes more about the *dos* rather than the *don'ts*, as Psalm 32:3-5 says:

When I kept silent, my bones grew old through my groaning all-the-day long. For day and night your hand was heavy upon me; my vitality was turned into the drought of summer. I acknowledged my sin to You, and my iniquity I have not hidden. I said, "I will confess my transgressions to the Lord," and You forgave the iniquity of my sin.

Pain

Has the pain in your life left you bound by chains of bitterness? The Lord wants to lose this burden. He wants you to forgive those who have hurt you. By His supernatural mercy, He wants to do a work in your heart. Let your tears flow and pour out your heart to Him. As you do, He will replace the hurt with His love and wholeness. He is the only one capable of this because He alone is faithful, pure, and good. He wants to heal you and grant you freedom!

One way to help let go of emotional pain is to write your prayers in a journal. Whenever I do this, it helps unravel my feelings and my communication with the Lord seems more concrete. Then as I read my Bible, I see more of the Lord's clear answers to my questions. My journal entries usually end in thanksgiving because I discover His help.

Addiction is often disguised as an escape from a painful background. Issues with drugs, alcohol, sex, food, or gambling are all sin, but they usually exist when someone has difficulty facing their pain. After a person numbs their pain through addiction, chemical changes occur in the brain that trigger strong cravings for relief. Habit patterns develop to obey the call of sin. Yet simply knowing these facts doesn't help. To experience freedom, a miracle from God is needed. If this describes your experience, call out for His help! He wants to deliver you.

We've all heard of people who've been miraculously healed from addictions. I wish this was the case for everyone, but sadly, it's not. Most often, healing is a journey that takes time. Yet we can be assured that God is good. If we draw near to Him, He will draw near to us and bring the help we need. Often, He uses church or parachurch ministry groups for friendship and support. We need others in this painful life!

The Lord is the only one who is all loving and good. When we place our trust in people, we will be disappointed. Part of our healing is learning how to handle the pain that got us there in the first place. We must remember that He is the God of *all* comfort! Life is unfair and painful, but He desires for us to live in freedom and peace. Enjoying a daily, living relationship with Him is key for everything we face.

The more we see our need for Him, the more we come to appreciate what the Lord has saved us from. Those whose hurt is most severe can experience His comfort in greater measure. To find that comfort takes leaning on Him with everything we have. No one wants to hurt; in fact, we run from pain. Our pain may cause us to grow bitter, self-righteous, or even distant from God. Yet facing the truth behind it will free us. The truth remains that God loves us, He knows what's best for us, and even in our hardest trials, He will work things out for our good. The Holy Spirit is the God of all comfort, and He will heal in time as we give our burdens to Him.

Maybe your pain is physical. How do you cope with life, let alone maintain a relationship with God, with a debilitating ailment? Many people endure horrible pain for years, including my mother, who has crippling arthritis and Alzheimer's. Formerly an intelligent and compassionate Christian counselor, wife/mother/homemaker extraordinaire, and talented musician, she now spends her days staring at the walls or at people who walk by in the halls of her nursing home.

The simple act of getting out of bed is excruciating for my mother, having to transfer from her wheelchair with no strength in her legs or mobility in her joints. Her ability to read or comprehend Scripture is gone, and conversation confuses her. However, I can see the Lord carrying her through this time. When she hears a hymn, she remembers the lyrics and sings along. The sweetness of the Holy Spirit shines through her smile, and I've witnessed that even in this weakened state, her faith remains. The Lord's work remains when our works are done, and He alone is the author and perfecter of our faith. We can find hope in the fact that we are in His hands no matter what we go through in these failing bodies.

Though blind most of her life, Fanny Crosby became one of the most prolific hymn writers that ever lived. She could have felt sorry for herself and lived in obscurity, but instead she composed over 8,000 gospel songs, was a political activist, taught at a school for the blind, and became a public speaker and mission worker. It made her happy to know that when she got to heaven, the first thing she'd see would be Jesus' face. She thanked God for her blindness, knowing it gave her the opportunity for a more focused education and memory. Not many of us would wish for a trial like blindness, physical infirmity, or pain. But God can do a special work through those who accept their trial and suffering.

The Fear of Man

" The fear of man brings a snare, but whoever trusts in the Lord shall be safe." (Prov. 29:25)

We need discernment to keep our motives based in love. The fear of man comes from pride and from placing a high value on the opinions of people. As Christians in a dysfunctional society, we get caught up in trying to fit in. I used to think I had to live up to the expectations of others to be accepted. I thought being a servant meant always putting the needs of others before my own. Most of the time, I didn't even know what I wanted or needed.

Yet what is *God* calling us to do? He's asking us to live in His truth, and to do that, we must walk in the convictions He brings. Even when our obedience doesn't please those around us, pleasing God is our number-one priority. Jesus had some strong words for people-pleasers like me: "How can you believe, who receive honor from one another, and do not seek the honor that comes from the only God?" (John 5:44). By living in the truth, we please God and ultimately earn the respect of others.

How do we overcome the fear of man and learn to fear God instead? By taking our eyes off ourselves. Fearing God means living for a higher authority. It means relying on His Word and trusting in His goodness more than our circumstances. Loving ourselves doesn't boost our confidence, because we're weak and prone to fail. When we realize He is all-powerful, all-knowing, completely loving, and in control, it's easy to trust Him. God promises to never let us down. Isn't that better than feeling good about our own abilities and attributes? Real confidence comes from trusting Him and living by faith. And as a result, we come to know our Lord Jesus intimately.

Personally, knowing God's love changes us. As we abide in His Word daily, He changes us in every area. This is where our confidence comes from. God's love is more powerful than self-love because His perfect love casts out all fear. When we live in His love, there is no room for fear (I John 4:18).

To "arise and shine" as God commanded, we must acknowledge our need to repent, forgive, and trust Him by faith. We must believe that Jesus' power and love are at work in us. Don't wait until you "feel" it. Take a step of faith now by standing up straight and sharing His love with everyone around you. Keep your eyes on Him and let Him shine through you.

Darkness

People in the world walk in spiritual darkness, according to Isaiah 60:2: "For behold, the darkness shall cover the earth, and deep darkness the people." They walk *in the flesh*, and Galatians 5:19 tells us that the deeds of the flesh are evident, including "adultery, fornication, uncleanness, [and] lewdness." Some ideas of beauty get tangled up with these deeds of the flesh and are expressed in fashions. Clearly, the worldly woman's motivation to be beautiful is different than the godly woman's ideal.

Sadly, many women confuse beauty with sexual attraction, and they dress for immorality, impurity, and sensuality. Sensuality is a preoccupation with the pleasures of the senses, particularly sexual pleasure. Some women wear "body conscious" clothing to make themselves feel good. However, dressing sexy around anyone other than your husband does not communicate the Lord's glory. The beauty of a godly woman shines with the *Lord's* love and glory. An immodest woman, dressed in tight or revealing clothing, uses her God-given gift to gain attention, yet this gift is meant to be kept private for her husband. Clueless girls practice immodesty whether it's obvious, subtle, conscious, or unconscious. Modesty in all things is a sign of trusting God.

As women, our sexuality is a wonderful part of how God made us, and I don't believe He wants us to completely hide our bodies from the world. Yet some women take modesty too far by wearing only long smock dresses. Others hide their womanhood in masculine clothing. This may be a matter of conscience or personal preference, but if you are uncomfortable with your femininity, you may want to pray through any issues that could influence these feelings. Maybe you've suffered abuse, neglect, or ridicule in your upbringing. The Lord wants to help each one of us to dress and carry ourselves in purity.

Idols of wealth and greed have become a driving force in our society. Many women are bound by their desire for the latest fashions. Shopping is their passion and style is their god. In many circles, clothes and jewelry make a statement about social status, and acceptance is determined by dressing right. Don't fall into this trap. It's good to praise God for our blessings, but trusting in clothes for acceptance, power, or fulfillment is misplaced.

Idolizing fashion promotes envy, jealousy, and selfish ambition as we get caught up in unhealthy competition. Persuasive advertising tells us we need to measure up, and we're lured in by this message.

Some people dress for sorcery. This manifestation of the flesh has become less subtle recently with the increased popularity of satanic symbols on jewelry and clothing. The clothing of gang members and goths may reflect the rebellion, hatred, and strife they experience within.

The wardrobe of the flesh in Galatians 5 includes immorality, idolatry, and jealousy, which are all outward signs of our sinful nature. Women may demonstrate different combinations of these things. For example, the businesswoman who dresses a bit too sexy in her form-fitting silk blouse may want to appear superior to others in the office.

A great darkness covers the earth today. Hatred, self-worship, sexual impurity, and other poisonous fruits of the flesh infest people's lives, and the way we dress can reflect these sinful qualities. Instead of joining the fleeting fashion trends, ask the Lord to open your eyes to see the *new* set of clothes He has for you.

Glory

"But the Lord will arise over you." (Isa 60:2)

Ladies, we've been given an incredible gift. When we accept Jesus as our Savior, He places the glory of God upon us. But practically speaking, what *is* glory?

Other words for glory include illustrious, mighty, powerful, distinguished, splendid, majestic, and excellent. To have glory means to be honored, respected, ornamented, and celebrated. Glory shines with brightness, dignity, and nobility. Glory is magnificent and victorious, with extraordinary privileges and even a crown. Finally, glory is the light and splendor of the divine presence.

Being thought of as the best dressed or most accomplished woman at the office brings some fulfillment. However, that recognition can never touch our greater need for real love. Even if we receive man's accolades, we may still feel empty and alone.

Think of all the talented and attractive celebrities who have died an early death because of suicide or an overdose. For them, men's praises were not enough. Yet God gave His love by sending Jesus, His glory, to us. And we can lift our heads now because, as Isaiah 60:2 says, we are filled completely and surrounded by His love and grace. This is what we're designed for and looking for—He loves us! Because Jesus came to earth and offered His life as payment for all the wrong we've done, we can have a living and real relationship with God through simple faith in Him.

We once gained acceptance by means of the flesh, but through Christ we no longer need to do that. Jesus showed us how to live a radically different life. Instead of immorality, He lived in purity. Instead of self-absorption, He focused on others. Instead of greediness and materialism, He gave Himself to others and lived simply. Instead of practicing sorcery, He worshipped God in all His actions. Instead of living in competition, envy, jealousy, or selfish ambition, He laid down His life and became a servant. Instead of hatred, violence, or rebellion, He submitted to His Father. Finally, instead of revelry or drunkenness, He showed self-control. Jesus never sinned but reflected God's glory in everything He did. Think of how good Jesus is, and how He asks us to radiate His goodness and glory. And He wants to do this by living through us. Wow! That's something different.

When I was single, I used to think I'd feel confident if I had a boyfriend. I thought I'd lose all my insecurities and my need for acceptance, but that didn't happen. The reality is that all relationships can be selfish, no matter how wonderful the other person is. Haven't we *all* been selfish in relationships? The confidence we think we'll gain eludes us. How much more should a relationship with the God of the Universe give us true security and confidence? He is our rock. As the hit song recorded by Celine Dion says, "I'm everything I am because you loved me" (Diane Warren 1996, "Because You Loved Me").

Knowing the Lord has clothed us with His glory, why would we rely on our own abilities to bring the affirmation we desire? We already have all we need. Jesus loves us beyond comprehension. We are beautiful because He lives in us. His presence in our lives makes us radiant. Seeking Him, knowing Him through His Word, and loving Him as we abide in a living, daily walk with Him will cause us to shine and radiate His beauty to a dark world. Let's praise Him for all He's done!

For Discussion:

1. Think of a woman who shines with the Lord's glory and love. What qualities do you admire in her?

2. Have you ever been hindered by the fear of man? How might obeying the directive in Isaiah 60:1-2 free you from that fear?

3. How have you seen the beauty of the world as not so beautiful?

4. How can you "arise and shine" in practical ways this week?

5. What does it mean to radiate God's inner beauty?

6. How is the Lord's beauty different from arrogance?

For Prayer:

1. Confess your sins, big and small, to the Lord, knowing He will forgive and deliver you (I John 1:9). We all need a Savior!

2. Give your hurts and fears to God. Spend time with Him and let Him comfort you through His Word.

3. Pray for faith to arise and shine for Him. He is the author of our faith. Pray for perseverance to keep your eyes on Him, even in trials.

For Application and Homework:

1. Do you have good posture? If not, think about why, and practice your best posture this week.

2. Read Isaiah 60:1-2 several times and look for ways to reflect God's glory and love. Show this newfound beauty to your family, your neighbors, and those you work with. Be ready to share with your group a report of how it went.

Chapter Two

Garment of Salvation

"I will greatly rejoice in the Lord; my soul shall be joyful in my God; for He has clothed me with the garments of salvation." (Isaiah 61:10)

Certainly, our salvation is the most precious gift the Lord gives us. And what could be more special than a wedding gown? Several scriptures describe believers as the bride of Christ:

"Then I, John, saw the holy city, in the New Jerusalem, coming down out of heaven from God, prepared as a bride adorned for her husband" (Rev. 21:2 NASB).

"Let us be glad and rejoice and give Him glory, for the marriage of the Lamb has come and His wife has made herself ready." And to her it was granted to be arrayed in fine linen, clean and bright, for the fine linen is the righteous acts of the saints. Then he said to me, "Write: 'Blessed are those who are called to the marriage supper of the Lamb!'" And he said to me, "These are the true sayings of God" (Rev. 19:7-9).

We look forward to the coming marriage feast of the Lamb. Signs in the Bible indicate it may happen very soon. Matthew 22: 1-14 tells about a wedding celebration where many are invited but refuse to come. The servants of the master invite others from the streets, both good and bad, so the hall will be filled. In verses 11-14, the master comes in:

"But when the king came in to see the guests, he saw a man there who did not have on a wedding garment. So, he said to him, "Friend, how did you get in here without a wedding garment?" And he was speechless. Then the king said to the servants, "Bind him hand and foot, take him away, and cast him into outer darkness; there will be weeping and gnashing of teeth." For many are called, but few are chosen.""

Just as wedding clothes are required for this party, the Garment of Salvation is required for the coming marriage feast of the Lamb.

The kind of wedding gown Jesus speaks of is not from this earth. It's not available in shops or found in bridal magazines. We can't earn it. It can't be passed down through the family. God, our father, has purchased our gown with the highest possible price—the life of His Own Son. Through Jesus' death, we are forgiven and cleansed from all our sin and filth. He clothes us with a pure white wedding gown, our Garment of Salvation.

In the Bible, salvation is associated with great joy. The writer of our theme verse in Isaiah 61:10 proclaims, "I will greatly rejoice in the Lord, my soul shall be joyful in my God." Here are a few more scriptures about this garment:

"The king shall have joy in Your strength, O Lord; and in Your salvation how greatly shall he rejoice!" (Psalm 21:1).

"Restore to me the joy of Your salvation, and uphold me by Your generous spirit" (Psalm 51:12).

"But I have trusted in Your mercy; my heart shall rejoice in Your salvation" (Psalm 13:5).

Our salvation is meant to be a source of great joy. Is it? I don't know about you, but I take mine for granted most of the time. I seldom stop to think about how beautiful the Garment of Salvation really is. Scripture gives two reasons why salvation is a source of joy.

Here Comes the Bride

Being saved from sin brings us into relationship with God, a relationship that culminates in marriage at Christ's return (Revelation 19:6-9). Just as human love relationships give joy, so our love with the Lord gives much joy. While in college, I got engaged to be married and remember feeling so happy, as if in a daze. Most days were spent smiling and daydreaming about my fiancé, and I had difficulty studying.

If we are married, what we have with our husbands may be real and good, yet what we have with the Lord is even greater (though less tangible). We love Him so much because we have seen Him work in our lives. But even more wonderful is the fact that He loves us. He *is* the perfect husband—so much greater than any human. Looking at the qualities of a perfect husband, we see how the Lord exemplifies each one, as I John 3:1 says, "Behold what manner of love the Father has bestowed on us."

Qualities of a good husband

A good husband is a provider. God is our provider.

"And my God shall supply all your need according to His riches in glory by Christ Jesus" (Phil. 4:19).

We read in Genesis 22:14 that the very name of God, Jehovah Jireh, means "the Lord will provide." Many more scriptures speak of the Lord being our provider, including Nehemiah 9:15, Psalm 147:8, I Corinthians 10:13, and Hebrews 11:40.

A good husband is faithful. God is faithful.

"Kings shall see and arise, princes also shall worship, because of the Lord who is faithful, the Holy One of Israel; and He has chosen you" (Isa 49:7). See also Revelation 19:11, Deuteronomy 7:9, I Corinthians 1:9, I Thessalonians 5:24, I Peter 4:19, and I John 1:9.

The love of a good husband is lasting. God's love is everlasting. You will live together through eternity.
"Praise the Lord! Oh, give thanks to the Lord, for He is good! For His mercy endures forever" (Ps. 106:1).

See also Psalm 136, Deuteronomy 33:27, Isaiah 40:28, and Jeremiah 31:3.

The love of a good husband is unconditional. God's love is unconditional.

"For I am persuaded that neither death nor life, nor angels nor principalities nor powers, nor things present nor things to come, nor height nor depth, nor any other created thing, shall be able to separate us from the love of God, which is in Christ Jesus our Lord" (Rom. 8: 38-39). See also I Corinthians 13.

A good husband is caring. God is caring.

"Casting all your care upon Him, for He cares for you" (I Peter 5:7). See also Deut. 32:10.

A perfect husband is patient. God is patient.

"Love suffers long" (I Cor. 13:4).

A good husband is a companion and a partner. God is our companion and partner.

"For He Himself has said, 'I will never leave you nor forsake you.' So, we may boldly say: 'The Lord is my helper: I will not fear. What can man do to me?'" (Heb.13:5-6). See also Joshua 1:5, Ezra 9:9, Hebrews 13:5, and Deuteronomy 31:6, 8.

A good husband has passion in his love for you. He can't keep His eyes off of you. God is passionate in His love for you.

"For he who touches you touches the apple of His eye" (Zech. 2:8).

When Scripture speaks of you as the apple of His eye, it means that you are what He is looking at. The apple refers to the reflection you see of yourself as you gaze into someone's eye. See also Deuteronomy 32:10 and Psalm 17:8.

A good husband is full of compassion for you. God is compassionate.

"The Lord's lovingkindnesses indeed never cease, for His compassions never fail (Lam. 3:22 NASB). See also Deuteronomy 32:11, Nehemiah 9:17, Joel 2:13, Deuteronomy 4:31, Nehemiah 9:19, Lamentations 3:22, Matthew 9:36, and James 5:11.

A good husband loves you with a pure and undefiled love. God's love is pure.

"But with the precious blood of Christ, as of a lamb without blemish and without spot. He indeed was foreordained before the foundation of the world, but was manifest in these last times for you" (I Peter 1:19-20). See also I Samuel 2:2, Isaiah 6:3, Exodus 15:11, I Thessalonians 3:13, and Hebrews 12:10.

A good husband is a spiritual leader. God is our ultimate spiritual leader.

"Husbands, love your wives just as Christ also loved the church and gave Himself for her, that He might sanctify and cleanse her with the washing of water by the word" (Eph. 5:25-26).

Whether single or married, the Lord wants us to know His love in all these areas. There is much reason for joy in our relationship with Him. He is the lover of our souls! He loves us perfectly and completely.

It's Him

The second source of joy in our salvation is that He alone obtained it, and He completed it. There is nothing we can add. He paid the debt we couldn't begin to pay, He was our righteousness when we were unrighteous, and He loved us when we despised Him. He rescued us from hell! To all of this, our response is pure joy.

Trying to earn God's acceptance through religion steals our joy. Sometimes we attempt to make amends for sin or try right a wrong before going to Him first. But it never works because our efforts divert attention from His completed work. We begin our relationship with God in grace but think we must finish by striving in our flesh. The Galatians struggled with this too. Paul wrote the Galatian church a letter because teachers came into their fellowship saying they had to follow the law before God would accept them.

How many times do *we* take up the law too, in little ways? Perhaps we serve out of duty instead of love and worship. Or maybe we tend toward legalism because it gives us control.

I once saw the Pharisees as evil and abominable until I saw myself in them. When I take up the law and think I can please God on my own, I lose the joy of living in His grace. Good works are fine if they are done out of love and worship to Him. They are not so fine when we're striving to gain His approval. We're already approved through Jesus' righteousness alone, and we can rest in that.

Realizing what God saved us from gives great joy. Our sin had us on a highway straight to hell, but the hand of God reached into our lives and saved us from that path. Sometimes we may feel righteous by thinking we have a handle on outward sins. We say to ourselves, *Certainly, I'm not as bad as criminals, murderers, or thieves.* Yet we forget how desperately we need a Savior.

It's healthy to confess our sins to God, no matter how insignificant we think they are. Scripture tells us to judge ourselves and take the log out of our own eye before removing the speck from our brother's. Often, it's the sins of others that bother us most—the sins we are prone to. We must humble ourselves and realize that from the beginning it was the Lord Himself who caused us to see Him. All we can do is give Him glory because He has done it all.

Maybe you thought Christianity was about being a good person, and what you've read in this chapter is new to you. Would you like to have a relationship with the loving God who created you? He's made a way to know Him through His Son, Jesus Christ, and I invite you to put on His Garment of Salvation. You don't have to lose twenty pounds first—it will fit you perfectly! Simply ask Him to come into your heart to be your Lord and Savior, and He will.

Isaiah 61:10 says, "I will rejoice greatly in the Lord, my soul shall be joyful in my God; for He has clothed me with the garments of salvation."

For Discussion:

1. Why do we sometimes lose the joy of our salvation?

2. How do we try to win God's approval?

3. How has the Lord become your perfect heavenly husband?

For Prayer:

Ask the Lord to give you the joy of your salvation in greater measure.

For Homework and Application:

Write out your testimony. Recount what the Lord saved you from and why you are thankful.

Chapter Three

Garment of Praise

"He has sent me…to give them…the garment of praise for the spirit
of heaviness." (Isa. 61:3)

What a dazzling promise and incredible exchange—we are free! We
don't have to be burdened with the heaviness of sin and depression
any longer. Instead, we can live each day thanking and praising the
Lord. Clothed with the Garment of Praise, the world around us
notices our glow as if we're wearing a sequin gown. Just like a
glittery dress that reflects light everywhere, we can shine the light of
the Lord when we put on the Garment of Praise.

Here's another incredible promise for us beauty-conscious gals: "For
praise from the upright is beautiful" (Psalm 33:1).

Praise makes us more becoming and attractive. Certainly, it makes
us more pleasing to the Lord. Wouldn't He (and everyone else)
rather hear words of praise than grumbling, complaining, and
faultfinding? Wouldn't *you* find a person more beautiful if their
words were pleasant?

What prevents us from becoming people of praise? One barrier is a
"spirit of heaviness," a load of burdens we naturally carry that gets
heavier as we go through life. We become weighed down with the
hard stuff— heartache, sorrow, loneliness, affliction, illness, stress,
and our own weakness. Striving to be righteous or do good works
can make us feel like we're dragging. All the problems we carry,
whether they're ours or they belong to others, can make life feel
unbearably heavy.

The Lord promises to take all these burdens as we praise Him. The act of surrender is worship, because when we surrender, we acknowledge who He is. This doesn't mean we always receive a solution right away or even get the "why" of what we're going through. Some trials we won't understand until He returns. But realizing God has the big picture in view helps us understand that He's in charge and can do a much better job of orchestrating our lives than we can. Since our words echo our hearts, it's a heart change He desires—a faith overhaul. When we surrender our burdens to Him, He's able to work His will.

God only allows those things in our lives that He plans for us. This includes sorrow and suffering because growth rarely happens without them. Still, we know the Good Shepherd is leading and He does all things well.

We need to learn to praise Him in every situation. In Hebrew, the root words for "praise" include acclamation and honor. Praise means to extol or glorify, to express approval and admiration, offer grateful homage, and to applaud, commend, or laud.

Moments of Praise

Praise is always appropriate, and we are told to praise the Lord in all things. Do you find yourself in one of these scenarios today?

1. Praise Him when you're happy:

"Is anyone cheerful? Let him sing psalms" (James 5:13).

That's easy, right? Yet, sometimes we forget who brings the good times. It's always Him. A blessing is an invitation to see His love in a deeper way. Try responding to His gift with love in return, and you will grow more in love with Him. All good things come from above (James 1:17). A song comes from what occupies our hearts. May our songs be ones of praise and thanksgiving.

2. Praise Him for His power:

"For the Lord is great and greatly to be praised" (I Chron. 16:25).

Are you in need of a strong helper? Maybe you need someone you can rely on to get the job done, someone to trust with delicate situations. Praising Him for His power increases our faith as we acknowledge the absolute truth of his greatness.

3. Praise Him as King:

"'Praise our God, all you His servants, and those who fear Him, both small and the great!' And I heard, as it were, the voice of a great multitude, as the sound of many waters and as the sound of mighty thunderings, saying, 'Alleluia! For the Lord God Omnipotent reigns!'" (Rev. 19:5-6).

Do you need someone to be in charge of things? Someone to rule over your unruly situations? Praise Him because He is able. Jesus reigns in heaven, and He also wants to reign in you, doing all things for your good.

4. Praise Him for answers to prayer:

"Remember His marvelous works which He has done" (Psalm 105:5).

Has He answered any prayers for you lately? Think about what you were praying for last week. Have you seen Him act in your life? We are told to remember for a reason. Remembering answered prayers increases our faith and the faith of those around us, especially when we excitedly share His answers with others.

5.   Praise Him for His promises and His attributes:

 "God is love" (I John 4:8).

Maybe you've heard of a prayer format called *ACTS*, which is an acronym for **A**doration, **C**onfession, **T**hanksgiving, and **S**upplication. Using this tool helps us focus on the Lord's greatness (adoration), express our need for Him (confession), thank Him for His blessings (thanksgiving), and ask Him for our requests (supplication). Praying this way also increases our faith and gives us proper perspective. By the time we ask for requests, we find ourselves wanting His will more than anything else.

There's no religious formula for prayer, and there's always freedom. But remembering His attributes and promises as we pray is always helpful.

6.   Praise Him for your salvation:

 "I will greatly rejoice in the Lord; my soul shall be joyful in my God; for He has clothed me with the garments of salvation" (Isaiah 61:10).

Remember His sacrifice often. Remember what He saved you from and what you used to be. Praise Him always for your salvation.

7.   Tell His praise to others:

" Sing to Him, sing psalms to Him; talk of all His wondrous works!" (Psalm 105:2).

Praising God is a great witnessing tool. When He answers your prayers, tell others. It's a testimony to your friends and will increase their faith as well as yours. When you tell unbelievers what He's done for you, it encourages them to take a second look at the Lord and to go home and think about it. God is alive and working in His children's lives, so let's not be bashful about sharing Him. When the children of Israel stopped telling their sons and daughters about all the Lord's works and power, their children's hearts began to stray.

8.   Praise Him in trials:

"Therefore, by Him let us continually offer the sacrifice of praise to God, that is, the fruit of our lips, giving thanks to His name" (Heb.13:15).

Praising the Lord is easy when things go well. Yet God desires that we also praise Him when we're least capable. When we're completely drained of our own resources, praise is a sacrifice. This kind of praise is probably not a happy song—He doesn't ask us to be dishonest about how we feel. But He does want us to acknowledge His sovereignty and control over our circumstances, to surrender our questions, fears, and anger to Him in complete trust. When we lay it all at His feet, He carries the burden and we experience a peace that passes understanding.

9.   Praise Him in the assembly:

"Bless God in the congregations" (Psalm 68:26).

Praising the Lord with other Christians is vital for our faith. Hebrews 10:25 tells us not to forsake gathering together. We need encouragement from fellow believers to keep us on the right track and help us grow spiritually. Many Christians feel discouraged and hurt from bad experiences. They withdraw from fellowship and have church at home where they feel safe. However, there is no perfect church. God is the only perfect one, and Jesus is the only true head of the church. As His body, He has given us to each other for the long-term good of everyone. This gathering together is where we learn about His love. Yes, we may get hurt because the church is full of sinners (including you and me), but there is also great blessing if we obey and praise the Lord in fellowship with other Christians.

10. Join all creation in praising Him, as Psalm 148:1-10 declares:

"Praise the Lord! Praise the Lord from the heavens; praise Him in the heights! Praise Him, all His angels...hosts...sun and moon...stars of light...you, heavens of heavens...waters above the heavens....Praise the Lord from the earth, you great sea creatures and all the depths; fire and hail, snow and clouds; stormy wind...mountains and all hills; fruitful trees and all cedars; beasts and all cattle; creeping things and flying fowl."

On the very first Palm Sunday, Jesus said that if the people didn't praise Him, the rocks and hills would cry out. Everything was created for God's praise, including the mountains, trees, and water. Since I live in the beautiful Northwest, I love to hike in the mountains and watch waves at the beach. Everything is close by. The majesty of creation energizes me. The Lord's astounding power and creativity are ours to ponder. This kind of pondering inspired many early scientists in their discoveries.

You may remember the story of Sir Isaac Newton. As legend has it, he developed the theory of gravity after he was hit on the head by a falling apple. His attention to nature and his inquiring mind not only increased our understanding of gravity, but we also have him to thank for much of our knowledge of optics, sound, astronomy, and mathematics. Newton made such an impact on science that on his epitaph the English poet, Alexander Pope, wrote, "Nature and nature's laws lay hid at night; God said, 'Let Newton be' and all was light." As Proverbs: 25:2 reveals, "It is the glory of God to conceal a matter, but the glory of kings is to search out a matter."

Enjoy the spectacular fiery-pink sunrises and sunsets as His portrait of beauty and love to you. Lift your heart to Him in worship and praise for His creation.

11. Praise Him with everything you are:

 "Bless the Lord, O my soul; and all that is within me, bless His holy name!" (Psalm 103:1).

God created you to worship Him in your own unique way. There's no method or pattern you must follow. Worship and praise are an expression of love, and often the best way to show love is creative and spontaneous. He made each one of us special and different from every other person on earth.

Together we're like a gigantic orchestra with many instruments, and you're one of them. So, start playing your song—your high notes, your low notes, your complicated passages, and your simple melodies. There's no reason to hold back in any area because they're all beautiful to Him. He wants to hear the praise that only you can offer.

12. Sing praise to Him:

"Sing to Him, sing psalms to Him" (I Chron. 16:9).

Praise God for music! It can lift our spirit when we are down on strength. When we put praise to music, it's a double boost. Many of my mornings at home begin with listening to a worship music, and the songs get me through endless household tasks.

When I was pregnant with my third child, I developed complications that required bed rest. This was not easy, with two young children and an imminent move for our family. In addition, my husband had to dig a major drainage system before we could close the deal on our new home. But thanks to wonderful people in our church and family, I could stay on bed rest most of the time, and while I rested, I listened to Christian radio. Praising the Lord through music proved especially helpful in getting through this trial.

On Sunday mornings when my family went to church, the house was quiet and the radio station played only worship and praise songs. On those mornings, the Lord ministered to my heart, assuring me that He was my Father and was holding me in His hands. I can't explain what happened on an intellectual level, but my trust in Him strengthened. He knew I would need this assurance because I lost my baby at five months along. Praising Him through music became a source of great comfort, and it's still a vital part of my life today.

13. Praise Him out of love:

"You shall love the Lord your God with all your heart, with all your soul, and with all your strength" (Deut. 6:5).

There's so much to love about our Lord. He's incredible! Think about His love for you, and you will love Him more.

With so many reasons and ways to praise the Lord, let's drop those bulky old backpacks of worry. Hasn't controlling things been tiring? No wonder the spirit of heaviness is also called a spirit of fainting (NASB). Instead, the Lord wants to give you a stunning, shiny gown of praise—what a great exchange! Praise the Lord!

For Discussion:

1. What is your favorite way to praise the Lord?

2. When is it hardest for you to praise Him? Why?

For Prayer:

1. Ask God to help you praise Him in every circumstance with all your heart.

2. Include a time of adoration in your daily prayer time. Choose an attribute of God to meditate on. Let Him expand your view of Him.

For Homework and Application:

1. Read Psalm 103 and list the different ways the author praises God; for example, "He forgives all my sins."

2. After reading the psalmist's reasons for praising the Lord, write down your own reasons.

3. Practice praising the Lord in every situation, and take notice of how it lightens your load.

Chapter Four

Robe of Righteousness

"He has covered me with the robe of righteousness." (Isa. 61:10)

How luxurious to be wrapped in a warm, cozy fur coat! A woman makes a statement when she's out on the town wearing a floor-length fur. These coats are a luxury, usually for the wealthy, and we're not talking about the faux variety. When someone wears a long fur coat, people may think, s*he must be important* or *there goes a movie star*! The lives of many flawless animals are required for this special article of clothing, and the monetary sacrifice to purchase a quality fur is phenomenal. Yet the cost pales in comparison to God's sacrifice for us. When clothed in His righteousness, we're similarly surrounded by a warm and comforting peace. He chose to give His Only Son, Jesus, to die and pay the penalty for our sin. When we were sinners and didn't even know we needed Him (and actually were His enemies), He showed His love for us, according to Romans 5:8.

Today, fur coats are unpopular with animal activist groups, and in the eyes of the world, righteousness is also unpopular. But those who endure the scorn of the world and wear His robe of righteousness will also wear it in eternity (Rev. 7:9).

Where did it all begin?

Let's look at Genesis 3:7-11 to see the first robes of righteousness. After Adam and Eve ate the fruit God told them not to eat, they found out they were naked:

"Then the eyes of both of them were opened, and they knew that they were naked; and they sewed fig leaves together and made themselves coverings. And they heard the sound of the Lord God walking in the garden in the cool of the day, and Adam and his wife hid themselves from the presence of the Lord God among the trees of the garden.

Then the Lord God called to Adam and said to him, "Where are you?"

So, he said, "I heard Your voice in the garden, and I was afraid because I was naked; and I hid myself."

And He said, "Who told you that you were naked? Have you eaten from the tree of which I commanded you that you should not eat?"

Fig leaves for clothes? Those don't sound comfortable (probably on the itchy side). It's inferred in this passage that the leaves didn't even work because when God came to find Adam and Eve, they were still naked and hiding. Fig leaves represent the ways we try to cover our own sin. Have you ever noticed how kids sometimes try to hide what they've done? They're not good liars. When mine were little, I used to wonder where all the candy from the candy dish went since my kids said they didn't eat it. But for one of them, the chocolate evidence was smeared all over his mouth. Hiding from God is much like that. It never works.

In Genesis 3:21 we see God's love for Adam and Eve expressed: "Also for Adam and his wife the Lord God made tunics of skin, and clothed them." Animals had to die for the clothing to be made. Blood had to be shed to make Adam and Eve presentable before God and to hide their shame and nakedness. Of course, we know that it was only a temporary fix. They died spiritually and lost their unhindered access to God. They had to leave the Garden of Eden, to live under the curse, and eventually die physically. But God, in His mercy, provided for them so they didn't have to hide in the bushes for the rest of their lives.

Jesus, the Ultimate

Jesus provided the ultimate sacrifice so we could be made presentable before God. Through His death, He purchased for every believer a robe of righteousness. Isaiah 61:10 says that He has wrapped us in that robe. Isn't that good to know? Not just shorts and a T-shirt, but a head-to-floor fur coat. I, for one, need it. His righteousness covers all my sins—my selfishness, wrong words, actions, thoughts, and even those things I'm not aware of or try to hide.

We deserve to be punished. We're guilty of sin, but by God's mercy He sees us as more than just innocent—He sees us as righteous because of Jesus. Being innocent is neutral. Being righteous indicates a positive position. The only way this is possible is by Jesus living in us, loving others and doing good things through us. As we learn about the other garments and the qualities they represent, we'll see the outworking of this and discover the many facets of His love.

Heavenly Clothing

Growing up in Sunday school, I was confused about an issue. I thought that since Adam and Eve were naked before the fall (remember all the pictures?), we would no longer need clothes after Jesus' second coming. Being a modest little girl, this thought terrified me. Later I learned the promise in Revelation 7:9 about the robe of righteousness given to each saint in God's kingdom. Whew, what a relief! Even in heaven we will wear this robe.

Romans 3:23 says, "For all have sinned and fall short of the glory of God." No one on earth can make it to heaven on their own. Everyone is guilty of sin. Even the finest seamstress would be unable to fashion a garment that could cover every flaw. Hebrews 9:22 tells us that "according to the law almost all things are purified with blood, and without shedding of blood there is no remission." Jesus paid such a dear price for us to be presentable to God, and He's clothed us in His own life. We stand before God only in Him, wrapped head to toe with Jesus' righteousness, which covers all our sin.

Righteousness and Peace

How do we see this righteousness and know its practical effect in our lives? Isaiah 32:17-18 says, "The work of righteousness will be peace, and the effect of righteousness, quietness and assurance forever. My people will dwell in a peaceful habitation, in secure dwellings, and in quiet resting places." Psalm 72 also links peace and righteousness. Just as joy is a by-product of our salvation, so peace is a by-product of our righteousness.

Recently during a stressful conflict with a friend, I prayed the Lord would show me how this truth about peace and righteousness could be true. I didn't see how peace was possible until the conflict was resolved because whatever I did to try to fix it, it seemed worse. One night I was lying in bed on my lambskin rug, praying and reading. The Lord showed me that in human relationships there is always a certain amount of give and take, but with the Lord we're accepted just the way we are. There's no work involved in maintaining our relationship with Him, and it doesn't matter how pretty, witty, fun, caring, warm, or capable we are (or aren't). We can rest knowing we're completely accepted because He covers us with Jesus' righteousness. When God looks at us, He sees the beauty and holiness of Jesus.

As I lay on my cozy lambskin, I started thinking about His love and what it means to be loved unconditionally, like being wrapped in a warm fur and totally resting. Those thoughts immediately caused my heart to worship and thank Him, and soon I peacefully dozed off to sleep. The next day the conflict with my friend resolved. It was interesting to me that even in the middle of something so stressful, I experienced peace by acknowledging His righteousness and accepting that righteousness in my life.

When we realize His righteousness for ourselves and let Him clothe us with His robe, we can have peace. We don't have to strive to be liked anymore! We can drop the insecurity we've held onto since adolescence. We are loved and accepted exactly the way we are by the one who matters most. Believe this for your life.

Righteousness is not something we clothe ourselves in; it's a gift from God alone. The self-righteousness of Christians through the ages has brought much grief and destruction. Those who think they are the moral instructors to society should button their lips. People need to see the Lord Jesus and *His* righteousness in our lives, not the sham of our own righteousness. We are weak. He is strong. We are sinful but forgiven, and He is the Holy One. When we live honestly before others, then they can see Jesus and His righteousness.

Isaiah 64:6 says, "All our righteousnesses are like filthy rags." The righteousness He wants to see in us is from Jesus alone. When we try to be righteous to gain His approval, it never works. In fact, it's as if He says, "Don't bother; that's ugly compared to what I can give you." So, accept the beautiful fur coat He offers and rest in it. Rest in *His* righteousness.

For Discussion:

1. How does righteousness bring peace?
2. What is a righteous person like?

For Prayer:

1. Pray that you experience the peace of God that comes from being wrapped in the Robe of Righteousness.

2. Spend time praising the Lord for His righteousness, given to you.

For Homework and Application

1. Read Psalm 72 and write out three promises of peace for the righteous:

Chapter 5

The Garment of Compassion

"Therefore, as God's chosen people, holy and dearly loved, clothe yourselves with compassion." (Col 3:12 NIV)

In Colossians 3:12 we find a store full of lovely and practical pieces for our spiritual wardrobe. First, we'll look at the Garment of Compassion. Think of it as a pair of smooth pajamas, a soft robe, and furry slippers—what someone might wear when caring for a baby or young child in the middle of the night. Whether it's a 2 a.m. feeding, a nightmare, or teething pain, being cradled in Mommy's arms in the rocking chair is what's needed to soothe the pain or fear, and help a child return to sleep. The spiritual Garment of Compassion does the same for those around us. A soft, reassuring word or touch is so comforting to a soul in need.

The Compassion of Jesus

Compassion is one of Jesus' attributes. The Gospels show numerous examples of Jesus acting when He was "moved with compassion."

In Matthew 15:32, Jesus was moved with compassion when He and his disciples fed the crowd of 4,000 and met their physical needs.

In Matthew 20:34, Jesus touched the eyes of two blind men and healed them. Again, He was moved by compassion, not by pride or the desire for fame. Unfortunately, this isn't always the case in healing meetings. Jesus' love and compassion is where *true* healing takes place—physical, emotional, and spiritual.

In Matthew 18:27, the master in this parable (a type of Jesus) was moved with compassion to forgive the debt of his servant. God's forgiveness, too, comes from compassion, and it's with His compassion that we're able to forgive others.

In Matthew 9:36, Jesus saw the people's need for leadership and encouragement. Out of compassion, He told His disciples to pray that the Lord would send workers to meet those needs. Notice that power trips or ego had nothing to do with His response. Prayer, evangelism, and the call to spiritual leadership were all prompted by Jesus' compassion.

Compassion means to show kindness or assistance, to suffer with another, to be touched, to have pity, to experience distress through the ills of others, and to be moved to act.

A New Outfit

Colossians 3:12 commands us to be clothed with compassion. There's a certain amount of human compassion we can have naturally. Parents usually have it for their children, and some careers like nursing or counseling attract people with this quality. But the Garment of Compassion Jesus has for us is supernatural. In some Bible translations compassion is called "tender mercies." God's compassion is big enough to reach beyond limited resources and touch a hurting world, and the only way to have more is to ask Him. He wants to supply it.

Often as I prepare to minister in prisons, I ask God to give me His love for the inmates, because I don't have it naturally. I don't know these people, and if God hadn't led me into this ministry, I wouldn't have chosen to meet them. But I know God loves them and longs to show them His love and help. Preaching and sharing will do nothing unless Jesus' love is with me, motivating every word. As I feel His love come into my heart, I find that by the end of the ministry time I'm sad to leave, and I come away deeply concerned for the new friends I've made.

Jesus' compassion working through us can do wonderful things. So, go and get your soft pajamas on!

For Discussion:

1. Jesus' compassion moved Him to action. What are some practical things *you* can do to show His compassion?

2. Specifically, who can you do these things for?

For Prayer:

1. Pray for a heart of compassion for those in your world this week.

2. Pray to see Jesus' compassion as He ministers through you.

3. Spend time thanking the Lord for His compassion toward you.

For Homework:

1. Read Lamentations 3:21-25, and tell about a time in your life when you saw God's unfailing compassion.

2. How have you experienced His new mercies every morning?

3. Reflect on how the Lord has been your portion and given you hope.

4. Tell about a time when you saw God's goodness when you waited for Him.

Chapter Six

The Garment of Kindness

"Put on…kindness." (Col. 3:12) NKJV

What are the styles and fashions of kindness? One clothing piece to imagine is an apron. This garment can be worn when baking a treat for your family, like a favorite pie or cake for no special reason. It can be worn to make a surprise for a neighbor or friend who needs to be encouraged. Maybe you'll put on this apron when making a meal for a new mother or for someone who's suffering with illness. It can also be worn when preparing food to share with a family in financial need. As you can see, the uses for the Garment of Kindness are many.

Of course, kindness is a welcome quality outside the kitchen as well. Recall the things God has done in your life that have left you awestruck. That's His kindness. Let's look at how Jesus demonstrated kindness.

A Non-Random Act of Kindness

There's a story in the Bible about a man who experienced the Lord's overwhelming kindness. You may remember the Sunday school song about him--his name is Zacchaeus. Read his story in Luke 19:1-10:

"Then Jesus entered and passed through Jericho. Now behold, there was a man named Zacchaeus, who was a chief tax collector, and he was rich. And he sought to see who Jesus was, but could not because of the crowd, for he was of short stature. So, he ran ahead and climbed up into a sycamore tree to see him, for he was going to pass that way. And when Jesus came to the place, He looked up and saw him, and said to him, "Zacchaeus, make haste and come down, for today I must stay at your house." So, he made haste and came down, and received Him joyfully. But when they saw it, they all complained, saying, "He has gone to be a guest with a man who is a sinner." Then Zacchaeus stood and said to the Lord, "Look, Lord, I give half of my goods to the poor; and if I have taken anything from anyone by false accusation, I restore fourfold." And Jesus said to him, "Today salvation has come to this house, because he also is a son of Abraham; for the Son of Man has come to seek and to save that which was lost."

First, we see that Jesus' kindness went beyond what was expected. Zacchaeus was just hoping to *see* Jesus. But Jesus said, "Let's do lunch." He was a guest in Zacchaeus's home, which was something done only with good friends. Kindness considers others and seeks out ways to show love and meet needs.

Secondly, kindness isn't prejudiced. Zacchaeus wasn't just a tax collector, he was a *chief* tax collector. He made his living by cheating people—namely, those around him in Jericho, The Jews avoided Zacchaeus and considered him a repulsive sinner. And though Jesus was well aware of these social barriers, He reached out to him publicly.

We need to be careful not to let pride and prejudice hinder us from being kind. Perhaps we don't consider ourselves prejudiced, but how often do we let differences in social status, age, or physical appearance separate us from others? We usually hang out with friends who are most like us. Personally, I have limited bandwidth for including others who don't fit my comfort zone. Yet I'm missing out on some great friendships and opportunities when I'm in that mindset. Let's break out of our cliques and open our arms to others.

The third thing we see from this story is that Jesus' kindness leads to repentance (Rom. 2:4). Zacchaeus was so touched when Jesus reached out to him that he repented immediately. Jesus never had to say, "Hey! It's time to clean up your life, Buddy." When His lovingkindness touches someone's life, they *want* to change.

Bring Kindness Home with You

I was once part of a prayer group that met weekly to pray for our kids and their schools. A new woman moved to the area and joined our group, and she had a baby soon after she joined. Some women organized a schedule of bringing meals to help during her recovery. She hadn't found a church yet, and we were the only Christians she knew. If someone hadn't suggested taking her meals, I probably would have simply congratulated her. After all, I didn't even know her last name. Apparently, this woman was so touched by our group reaching out that she began to be healed from a hurtful situation she'd experienced in her previous location. Even in this small example, the Lord's kindness was evident. Whether experienced directly from Him or through the body of Christ, His kindness considers others and shows love that goes beyond what's expected. It isn't prejudiced or partial, even when people are new, and His kindness leads to changed hearts.

We all probably know at least one person who is especially blessed with a heart full of God's kindness. I'd like to tell you about Mary Lou, who I met at my church in the mid-nineties. She approached me warmly, shook my hand, and genuinely said how nice it was to meet me. As I got to know her, she and her husband showed interest in the music ministry my husband and I were involved in, and they even attended one of our performances.

Although she had a new baby at the time and more children than I did, she invited us to her home for dinner. I felt blessed to know her, and I noticed her kindness toward everyone. At our women's Bible study, she welcomed new people and expressed extra care to those who carried burdens, not showing partiality in any way. She put all her energy into caring for others. Not long after meeting her, the Lord called her and her husband to full-time missionary work in Russia. We were sad to see her go. It was obvious why the Lord wanted to use her to extend His kindness to others. It showed me the need for all of us to carry on her example.

Consider the many ways Jesus has been kind to you and begin writing a list. As you ponder His kindness, let your heart respond to Him in worship. Knowing His kindness on a personal level will expand your heart to show it to others.

People need to see the Lord's kindness operating in our lives. Let's pray for His eyes to see those He wants us to touch with kindness. Look for the Zacchaeuses around you, and then pray for the Lord's ability to carry out deeds that will bless them. Maybe it's baking for someone or giving a gift. Or perhaps it's a phone call, a smile, a note, or a nice comment to someone who's not expecting it.

Proverbs 19:22 says, "What is desired in a man [and a woman] is kindness." Kindness is a lovely garment to wear.

For Discussion:

1. Describe a time when God used someone to show His kindness to you. How did it make you feel?

2. Share a form of prejudice you've seen or experienced. Tell why this barrier exists and how to overcome it in a practical way.

For Prayer:

Pray that God will reveal His kindness to you in a fresh way this week. Ask Him to bring you an opportunity to share His kindness with someone.

For Homework and Application:

1. Read the story of Dorcas in Acts 9:36-42. Dorcas was so kind that her friends could not accept her death.

2. Also read Proverbs 11:16 and Proverbs 31:26. Describe someone you know who has been full of kindness toward you. (Maybe they've made you feel welcome in a new situation or reached out with hospitality.)

3. From the examples above, list two qualities you admire and would like to implement in your own life with God's help.

1)

2)

Chapter Seven

Garment of Humility

"Be clothed with humility." (I Peter 5:5)
"Put on…humility." (Col. 3:12)

Humility must be doubly important since we are told twice in Scripture to be clothed in it. Think of the Garment of Humility as plain work clothes—sweats and jeans. There's certainly nothing flashy about this outfit, nothing to draw attention. A person in this garment is ready to get in there and do what needs to be done. Humility Helen, with hair pulled back and sponge in hand, is prepared to get at those hard-to-clean areas of life. In the process, she might rub up against some grimy stuff, but she knows that the water of the Word can wash the filth away.

Perhaps you're wondering, *why are work clothes part of our wardrobe?* It's because the humble, behind-the-scenes work is vital in keeping everything else together. Without this preparation, it would be like a high fashion model who didn't bother to shower before a show. It wouldn't matter how fancy her clothes were if she had dirty fingernails and greasy hair. Or like a house full of expensive furniture with floors that were never swept, bathrooms that were never scrubbed, and furniture that was never dusted. It would not be pretty! The humble work of maintaining a home keeps it presentable. In the same way, deeds done in humility are foundational to true beauty.

Sometimes humility can seem frightening and threatening. We're afraid to go unnoticed or worried that we'll be taken advantage of. Yet when we consider the example of Jesus, we see that humility is a precious garment.

Seven Lessons of Humility

Read the story of Jesus washing His disciples' feet in John 13:1-20:

"Now before the feast of the Passover, when Jesus knew that His hour had come that He should depart from this world to the Father, having loved His own who were in the world, He loved them to the end.

And supper being ended, the devil having already put it into the heart of Judas Iscariot, Simon's son, to betray Him, Jesus, knowing that the Father had given all things into His hands, and that He had come from God and was going to God, rose from supper and laid aside His garments, took a towel and girded Himself. After that, He poured water into a basin and began to wash the disciples' feet, and to wipe them with the towel with which He was girded. Then He came to Simon Peter. And Peter said to Him, "Lord, are You washing my feet?"

Jesus answered and said to him, "What I am doing you do not understand now, but you will know after this."

Peter said to Him, "You shall never wash my feet!"

Jesus answered him, "If I do not wash you, you have no part with Me."

Simon Peter said to Him, "Lord, not my feet only, but also my hands and my head!"

Jesus said to him, "He who is bathed needs only to wash his feet, but is completely clean; and you are clean, but not all of you." For He knew who would betray Him; therefore, He said, "You are not all clean."

So, when He had washed their feet, taken His garments, and sat down again, He said to them, "Do you know what I have done to you? You call Me Teacher and Lord, and you say well, for *so* I am. If I then, your Lord and Teacher, have washed your feet, you also ought to wash one another's feet. For I have given you an example, that you should do as I have done to you. Most assuredly, I say to you, a servant is not greater than his master; nor is he who is sent greater than he who sent him. If you know these things, blessed are you if you do them.

"I do not speak concerning all of you. I know whom I have chosen; but that the Scripture may be fulfilled, 'He who eats bread with Me has lifted up his heel against Me.' Now I tell you before it comes, that when it does come to pass, you may believe that I am He. Most assuredly, I say to you, he who receives whomever I send receives Me; and he who receives Me receives Him who sent Me."

Jesus is the supreme creator of the universe and of every living thing. He rules as king of all kings. Yet it was the Father's will that the Son would walk on this earth and become one of us. Jesus didn't live His life here as a king but as a servant, even taking on the lowly servant's role of washing feet. This teaches us much about humility.

Pride waits to be served, but humility takes action to serve. In verse 5, Jesus pours water, takes a towel, and starts to wash his disciples' feet. He must have had it in His mind to serve the disciples this way. Do we sit around and wait for obvious opportunities to serve? Or do we *look* for opportunities—even plan them—and then expend the effort to become a humble servant?

Pride doesn't risk being looked down on, but humility takes that risk. Jesus willingly took the low position of a servant. The word *humility* means not proud or arrogant; to be low in rank, position, or status; to be low-lying, of low degree; or to have lowliness of mind. Jesus' humble actions were so contrary to human nature.

Kids play the game, King of the Mountain, and adults play it too, in subtle ways. We like to be recognized for our positions and accomplishments, and we often exempt ourselves from lower jobs. The risk in doing menial work is that people may think less of us. No one wants to be invisible, yet humility is willing to take that risk.

Pride withholds doing good to an enemy, but humility gives, even to those who use you. Jesus knew that Judas would betray Him. In verse 18, Jesus quotes from Psalm 41:9: "Even my own familiar friend in whom I trusted, who ate my bread, has lifted up his heel against me." It's interesting that Jesus quoted this passage when he was in a vulnerable position—on the ground washing feet. He acted in love, even toward Judas, the one whom Jesus said had lifted his heel against Him. And Judas responded to that love by betraying Jesus. How painful this must have been! Humility bears the pain of serving those who take your service for granted or don't understand it. But to be clear, this isn't about taking abuse. It's about being a servant through Christ's love, even toward those who treat you like one. If you are in an abusive situation, get out of it immediately!

Humility is honest and completely transparent. Pride puffs itself up with inflated opinions of oneself, which are lies. *False* humility is pride in disguise, when people talk down about themselves to receive affirmation. Another form of false humility is when a person holds back from obeying a call on their life. They seem afraid to fail or to take risks, when the truth is that they're protecting their pride. When Jesus served, He didn't puff Himself up or deny His position and honor. In John 13:13, He showed His disciples that He is Lord, but also that the Lord serves others. Humility doesn't concern itself with rank; it serves with no apologies.

Humility is a mark of Jesus' servants. In John 13:16, Jesus reminds his disciples, "A servant is not greater than his master." In the same way that Jesus washed their feet, we should also show humility as servants to each other. Sadly, it isn't always true, but humility and service to others should be distinguishing characteristics of Christians.

Christian leaders, too, should be humble. In Luke 22:25-26, Jesus said, "The kings of the Gentiles exercise lordship over them, and those who exercise authority over them are called 'benefactors.' But not so among you; on the contrary, he who is the greatest among you, let him be as the younger, and he who governs as he who serves." When Jesus washed the disciples' feet, He gave them an example to follow: He was their leader, yet He was also their servant. As Christians, we may have opportunities to lead others too, and when this happens, we must remember that humility through serving makes a good leader.

You are saved by receiving Jesus' humble service to you. John 13:8-20 refers to this when the Lord tells Peter he must receive the service Jesus was doing. Christianity is about what God has done for us, not what we've done for Him. The Lord saved us (or bathed us, as he refers to it here). He also forgives us daily (or washes our feet). We are saved through His humility, and it's His humility that maintains our relationship with Him. All we can do is respond in worship. As we worship, we live our lives with the Garment of Humility on—humility back to Him and to the world around us. For more about Jesus' humility, read Philippians 2:6-11.

There are glory-filled jobs and not so glorious jobs, but both are necessary. For example, consider a TV talk show with two co-hosts who get all the glory. They are the personalities of the show, and their popularity determines whether the show succeeds or fails. But these stars wouldn't have their jobs unless there were also camera operators, a television network, corporate sponsors, directors, hair stylists, make-up artists, wardrobe people, facility maintenance, and design personnel.

At times, we all must be the unseen people who work for the good of all. The few times when we have a little spotlight may be fun (or maybe not), but in the real world we need to do the dishes, clean the toilets, type the memos, or whatever other lowly jobs need to be done. Knowing that Jesus humbled Himself to reach us, how can we respond to Him any other way? Wearing the Garment of Humility is much like wearing work clothes. It won't draw the glamorous attention our flesh seeks, but it will help us accomplish things for the Lord that can't be done any other way.

For Discussion:

1. Housecleaning clothes might be one form of the Garment of Humility. What's another clothing possibility for this attribute? Explain your answer.

4. Is humility scary to you? If yes, tell why.

5. One definition of humility is to have an honest view of yourself. How is this true?

For Prayer:

1. James 4:6 says, "God resists the proud, but gives grace to the humble." Pray that the humility of Jesus would be a part of your being.

2. Ask the Lord to reveal any areas of pride in your heart. When He does, repent of them.

3. Pray for the courage to serve others.

For Homework and Application:

1. Read Proverbs 15:33 and Philippians 2:3-4. List three things you notice about humility in these passages:
   1)
   2)
   3)

2. Do something you don't have to do and that no one else wants to do, either at home or at your job. Tell what you did. How did you feel about it? Describe any reaction you may have received from others.

Chapter Eight

The Garment of Gentleness

"Clothe yourself with…gentleness." (Col. 3:12 NIV)

Don't you love putting on a warm, cozy sweater on a frosty morning? All day, the sweater's warmth and softness bring you comfort. My favorite sweaters are cashmere or angora. The Garment of Gentleness is as soft as an angora sweater. It's never rough or abrasive, never scratchy or irritating. The inside of this sweater feels soft next to the skin, and it also feels soft to anyone who encounters it. The garment even softens the face of the person wearing it. Gentleness is a powerful quality that goes beyond feeling warm and fuzzy.

The American church witnessed an incredible revival in the nineties, when Promise Keepers called men to openly repent of their sins as husbands, fathers, and neighbors. Who could have predicted that stadiums full of men would gather, not at a sporting event but at an event with the sole purpose of returning to God? The way God worked was awe-inspiring. This much-needed revival has carried on, with many Christian men continuing to serve, bless their families, and pass down godly habits to their sons.

I believe women need a similar revival. Some women, swayed by feminist ideals, feel entitled in their homes and workplaces, expecting men to serve and carry equal loads of the housework. They believe a woman's role is to be pampered. Of course, the way a home is managed is up to each married couple, but Proverbs 31 and Titus 2 both give a biblical precedent for women to manage their homes.

Many of us have traded in our soft gentleness sweaters for porcupine coats of contention and strife. We've forgotten that the Lord sees a gentle and quiet woman as precious (I Peter 3:4). Out of fear, we've taken matters into our own hands and lost our place as our husband's helpers. When we could have been encouraging our men to become all God wants them to be, we've been self-centered and critical instead. Our prideful opinions and desire for control have discouraged men in their leadership. Not only are women short tempered and exacting in their homes, but also in business, where they can be more cutthroat than men, and where gentleness is often seen as weakness. How we need to repent and ask God to change us with a spirit of gentleness!

The Little Foals

We see the gentleness of Jesus in the account of the triumphant entry: "Say to Daughter Zion, 'See, your King comes to you, gentle and riding on a donkey, on a colt, the foal of a donkey'" (Matthew 21:5 NIV).
Perhaps you've wondered why this story is called "the triumphant entry." What was Jesus' triumph? Certainly, our humble king was praised as king in Jerusalem, but He also triumphed in the way He revealed who He was when He entered that city. By displaying gentleness over force, he showed an example of approachability.

Have you ever watched a US President arrive into town, either in person or on TV? The President pulls up in an elaborate limousine and stays in a fine hotel, surrounded by an army of bodyguards. It's a big deal to everyone! Our President needs a police blockade to ensure protection and distance from the crowds. What a difference from the way Jesus arrived into town! He allowed others to touch Him, even when He was in enemy territory. Worldly leaders may bring an army to force and intimidate people into obedience, but Jesus never forced anyone to do anything. He didn't even force the foal He rode on to leave its mother (both were there, according to Matthew 21:5). What a picture of gentleness!

A woman dressed in the Garment of Gentleness never forces or manipulates others. She's easy to get along with, polite, and peaceful. She offers opinions with sweet reasonableness, allowing freedom and grace to others even when there are differences of opinion. In a heated discussion, her gentle answers calm the angry quarreler, as Proverbs 31 describes: "A soft answer turns away wrath."

A gentle woman is pleasing to the Lord. I Peter 3:4: says, "Let [your adornment] be the hidden person of the heart, with the incorruptible beauty of a gentle and quiet spirit, which is very precious in the sight of God." She grows in confidence in her God, who bears her burdens and fights her battles. She is soft and tender toward others, making room for the little foals they might have in their lives. What are the foals in people's lives? Maybe they are the little children who are always on their mother's mind. Moms need to consider their children before making commitments to serve in any capacity. Or maybe a woman has problems below the surface or secret burdens she is carrying. Gentleness is not weakness; it is controlled strength. It takes great strength to *not* take control or react in anger but to respond with patience, kindness, and grace.

The opposite of gentleness is contention. The Bible describes the contentious woman in Proverbs 19:13, 21:19, and 25:24. These verses scare me. I never want to fight with anyone or be the constant drip torture woman that drives my husband to live in the desert or on a corner of the roof. A woman clad with contention is incited by a sideways glance, sees others as rivals, manipulates to get her way, and wrangles through conflicts. Have you ever been there?

There is hope! The Lord is always ready to help us. When we feel fury flaming up, ready to burn someone (the dragon lady syndrome), or we're tempted to verbally lash out at a family member, God wants to give us resources to draw from. He wants to help us stop, step back, pray—and when we feel rational again—to express our feelings calmly. If you are dealing with an adult, this is all you can do. If you are a parent or teacher dealing with children, some discipline might be called for, but never in a brawling or contentious manner.

If you 're dealing with an issue in gentleness and truth, and it's still unresolved, commit it to the Lord in prayer. The flesh might come in and start nagging you to take charge again and solve issues in your own strength. But let it go and let God do what He wants to do. His solution will be far better than the one you think you must have. He sees the big picture of our lives, and when we have patience to trust Him and not fight it on our own, He will bring solutions in His own gentle way.

Maybe that house project you're waiting for your husband to finish can be completed by you. Be resourceful! Learn to use a screwdriver, wield a paintbrush, and take out the garbage yourself (what a thought!). Your example will probably inspire him to do his part and bring peace where there has been strife. Your husband would love his home to be a place of rest instead of nagging, especially if he slays dragons at work all day. Okay, maybe it's not that life-threatening, but dealing with dissatisfied customers all day can be draining.

Even in relationships that aren't necessarily tense, I see women who can't seem to exist without everything going their way. Can we learn to let things go? Can we let our husbands or male bosses be the leaders (when appropriate) and not challenge their every word and action? Life is better if we learn to trust God with the control.

When in a public place, we often see the opposite of gentleness— perhaps a mother yelling at her kids or a wife bickering with her husband. In the marketplace, managers may bark at their employees and young women compete for male attention. This harsh communication shocks me—until I hear myself getting impatient with my husband or snippy with my friends. Not to mention my defensiveness when I'm criticized or corrected. Some reactions are so automatic. God help us!

Men are different from women, and women are different from each other. No one thinks or acts the same way. When others think differently, let's listen with respect and allow them the freedom to be who they are. Of course, we need to measure a person's example against God's Word before following their example, but for all those areas where the Lord allows us freedom, we should allow it to others. As our kids mature into adults, they need this from us. We need this in marriage as well, and in all healthy relationships. Let's drop our judgment, manipulation, and the other ways we try to control each other into "acceptable" behavior. Grace and trust are what Jesus is all about, and gentleness is a practical way to extend those heavenly qualities to each other.

II Timothy 2:24-25 says, "And a servant of the Lord must not quarrel but be gentle to all, able to teach, patient, in humility correcting those who are in opposition, if God perhaps will grant them repentance, so that they may know the truth."

For Discussion:

1. Being gentle means to not force or manipulate. Suppose you felt so strongly about something that you decided to fight for it. Is there a godly way to do this? Read II Corinthians 10:1 and explain how.

2. What do *you* do when you don't get your way? When others choose a different plan than yours, how do you deal with giving up control?

3. Describe the meaning of "sweet reasonableness" (Phil 4:5).

For Prayer:

Ask God to show you if you've controlled or manipulated others in the past. Repent and ask for His help to live in gentleness and freedom.

For Homework and Application:

List two personal situations and then tell how you might handle them in different ways, with either contention or gentleness.

Example:
Situation: *I disagree with my husband about a financial decision, and I know I'm right.*
Contention - *I yell to prove my point.*
Result - *disunity with husband, distance from God*
(Resolution is rarely found this way.)

Gentleness- *I pray, explain my viewpoint peacefully, submit to my husband, leave it in God's hands, and wait to see what happens without saying, "I told you so."*
Result- *peace, unity, love, support, and growth for both of us*

Fill in your own examples:
1) **Situation**:
    Contention -
    Result -
    Gentleness -
    Result -

2) **Situation**:
    Contention -
    Result -
    Gentleness -
    Result –

Chapter Nine

Garment of Patience

"Clothe yourself with...patience." (Col. 3:12 NIV)

I've never prayed for patience, but it seems the Lord wants to give me this quality anyway. I don't like long trials or challenging people and, of course, my way of thinking is "the right way." How dare others see things differently? Could my attitude be a sign that I do, in fact, need to be clothed with patience? The Colossians 3:12 wardrobe is not complete without it.

What a rare fashion piece, you say? In the flesh, it's impossible to afford! But take heart, the master designer Himself, the Holy Spirit, has tailored this garment just for us. It comes from His Fruit of the Spirit Collection. Think of this garment as a hand-knit sweater. Many long hours of work went into making this useful item, and it will keep you warm year after year through the cold winters. The Garment of Patience will also comfort you when unexpected, icy words come your way. Its warmth doesn't stop during the snow flurries and turbulent blizzards of life. By wearing the Garment of Patience, you will be made complete in all things and find favor with God (I Peter 2:20, James 1:4).

Here are some situations when we need to wear our patience sweaters:

1. **Patience during trials and waiting for answers to prayer**.
   There is no easy way through waiting; however, getting over the delusion that life should always go our way does help. As we

wait, we must remember God's promises and faithfulness to us. Thankfully, the Lord gives many scriptures to encourage us through these times. The following verses from II Peter 1:5-11 use the word *perseverance*, which means "patience in action":

"But also for this very reason, giving all diligence, add to your faith virtue, to virtue knowledge, to knowledge self-control, to self-control perseverance, to perseverance godliness, to godliness brotherly kindness, and to brotherly kindness love. For if these things are yours and abound, you will be neither barren nor unfruitful in the knowledge of our Lord Jesus Christ. For he who lacks these things is short-sighted, even to blindness, and has forgotten that he was cleansed from his old sins.

Therefore, brethren, be even more diligent to make your call and election sure, for if you do these things you will never stumble; for so an entrance will be supplied to you abundantly into the everlasting kingdom of our Lord and Saviour Jesus Christ."

A. We see here that the result of patience is knowing Jesus better.

B. James 1:2-4 tells us that the patience we gain in trials is given to build our faith: "My brethren, count it all joy when you fall into various trials, knowing that the testing of your faith produces patience. But let patience have its perfect work, that you may be perfect and complete, lacking nothing."

James 1:12 promises a crown of life to those who, through patience, endure to the end in their trials. God allows trials in our lives to increase our dependence on Him. Sitting back with patience through trials will draw us closer to Him. Real trust comes only with time. It's encouraging to know that every trial is allowed by God for our growth. Earthly possessions and comforts may be stripped away from us, but they are nothing compared to the glory and beauty to come. We're not forgotten by God, He allows no accidents, and His purpose will be accomplished through all that happens to us.

2. **Patience with those you teach.** This includes your children, your co-workers, and if you are a teacher, your students. Kids need to be taught the same thing over and over. I remember when my oldest son was 1½, he would toddle over to the stereo and fiddle with the dials every day, and each time I would direct him away. I know he got the message because he would always turn around first to see if I was looking. Finally, he understood that it was wrong to play with the stereo and stopped doing it. Now as a young adult, he doesn't play with it aimlessly anymore; he's constructive with his fiddling. As a successful computer engineer and musician, his curiosity is channeled to computers and music gear.

My piano students offer more ways to grow in patience. Some are very bright and don't need much help. When I explain something, they run with it. However, others don't get it. One student used to start a song on the wrong keys and never know it, throughout the whole piece. Sometimes I felt like giving up on him. But eventually, he learned to play a few songs competently. There's hope! Let's look at two scriptures about patience:

"Now we exhort you, brethren, warn those who are unruly, comfort the fainthearted, uphold the weak, be patient with all (I Thessalonians 5:14).

"Preach the word! Be ready in season and out of season. Convince, rebuke, exhort, with all longsuffering and teaching" (II Timothy 4:2).

Discipleship, the act of training someone in the ways of the Lord, is vital in the church. If you have known the Lord for many years, there are others who need to hear the wisdom you've gained. For example, a woman coming out of an abusive relationship needs constant assurance that God loves her and wants to heal her life. That healing comes through the patient teaching and encouragement of a friendship. As Christian women, we have a huge mission field in our own communities and have much to share with women who come out of abuse, broken homes, or human trafficking. Lord, use us to reach the broken women around us!

I Thessalonians 5:14 and II Timothy 4:2 specifically address patience in ministry. Teaching others about the God of the Bible is the most important thing we can share. This applies to any subject and any pupil we teach.

Having patience with someone doesn't mean correction is never needed. We are told to rebuke and exhort with great patience and instruction (II Tim. 4:2). We need to keep finding new tactics of teaching for those we instruct. Regarding my piano student, I needed to do things differently. I had to be more direct and use more ear training than I'd done with other students. When I implemented this training, I saw improvement. "The tongue of the wise makes knowledge acceptable" (Prov. 15:2 NASB).

What about those who don't know they need to be taught? I've seen young women who act like they know everything, and they scorn wisdom from those who are even a few years older. Sometimes I'd like to offer some unsolicited advice; I could save them a lot of pain! I've been there and done that with many of the same issues. Titus 2:3-5 tells us that older women can pray, offer gentle input, and teach younger women by example. Let's never stop learning from each other, and whatever our age, let's remain teachable.

3. **Patience when we are wronged** (when we're treated unjustly or someone hurts us). II Timothy 2:24-25 and I Peter 2:20 describe this kind of patience. In the Greek, the word *patience* means a combination of endurance and patience, so a better translation is "long-suffering." I Corinthians 13:4 says, "Love is patient" (NIV). My Bible cross-references here to I Peter 4:8: "And above all things have fervent love for one another, for 'love will cover a multitude of sins.'" Love gives us patience. If we're wronged by someone, what are our options? Revenge? Slander? Bitterness? It makes better sense to have patience and let God work things out.

   It's impossible to go through life without someone hurting us. I've had my share of hurt, and for me it's helpful to try and understand where the other person is coming from. Everyone has blind spots and everyone is selfish; we're all weak without the Holy Spirit's control. Even when we're wronged, God is still in control and He allows these situations for our growth. What can we do? Pray for God's love and patiently wait for His answer. True justice will happen in the end, often here on earth too. In the process, we'll grow up a little more.

4. **Patience when we're tense or in the middle of something painful**. If I'm stressed, I grow irritable with my family. I get distracted by trials and start taking them out on others. Here's a

story from Matthew 14:13 about a time when Jesus was in the middle of something hard and how He treated others with patient love:

"Now when Jesus heard it [news of John's death], He departed from there by boat to a deserted place by Himself. But when the multitudes heard it, they followed Him on foot from the cities. And when Jesus went out He saw a great multitude; and he was moved with compassion for them, and healed their sick."

Jesus wanted a break, but He couldn't even get a day off without everyone demanding more of Him. Right after healing those who were sick, He fed the 5000.

No doubt Jesus felt grieved over John's death. John was His partner in ministry, as well as his cousin. The Bible doesn't tell us how close they were, but John's death meant changes for Jesus. With his forerunner gone, Jesus knew His ministry had a timeline that culminated with His death. This realization must have been sobering. But even while Jesus dealt with these things, He still loved the people around Him and ministered to them. Like Jesus, we need patience with others, even when they're insensitive to what we're going through.

5. **Patience to learn a new skill and see a job to completion**. Having the end goal in view is helpful. When I was about 10 years old, my mom tried to teach me how to sew. She was a perfectionist, but I just wanted to get the project done as fast as possible. She'd often stop me and say, "You did this seam wrong. Now get the seam ripper out and do it over." Sparks would fly. Years later I talked to her about those sewing lessons. As she remembered it, I had taught myself how to sew!

Recently I made a sewing mistake by not following pattern instructions, and my inclination was to throw the half-finished blouse away rather than fix the problem. When I realized my response, I found it funny. I'm sure I could have benefited from listening to Mom a little more! Patience shown through diligence helps us learn new skills, and diligence pays off. The following verses illustrate this patient diligence:

"He who has a slack hand becomes poor, but the hand of the diligent makes rich" (Proverbs 10:4).

"The plans of the diligent lead surely to plenty, but those of everyone who is hasty, surely to poverty" (Proverbs 21:5).

Patience and diligence are needed for sanctification, which is the process of learning to walk closer to the Lord. It's disheartening to keep stumbling in the same mistakes, but don't give up! Stay on the path. Learning to walk His way takes practice, and as your teacher, Jesus never gets impatient. Keep your eyes on Him, the ultimate goal. He will hold your hand through the journey, instructing and encouraging you to the end.

One aspect of the Lord's patience is seen in His mercy. II Peter 3:9 says, "The Lord is not slack concerning His promise, as some count slackness, but is longsuffering toward us, not willing that any should perish but that all should come to repentance." We may get impatient waiting for Jesus to set up His perfect kingdom, but He has the bigger picture in mind. Perhaps He's waiting for one of our neighbors or an unsaved relative to come to know Him. In that patience, we can be glad.

II Timothy 2:12 reminds us that "if we endure, we shall also reign with Him." We know that our salvation is only by faith, not by works. We can't exert patience with fleshly power because it's part of our faith—the part that makes faith grow. This faith allows us to join the Lord Jesus in His suffering and helps us grow closer to Him. The love we have for others becomes more beautiful with patience woven into it. Be a warmer person by wearing the lovely, hand-knit Garment of Patience sweater from the Fruit of the Spirit Collection, found exclusively at Galatians 5th Avenue stores.

For Discussion:

1. How does patience make you complete in all things?

2. In what three areas of your life do you need patience?
    1)
    2)
    3)

3. How do you find help in the scriptures listed in this chapter?

For Prayer:

1. Pray about your heart's reaction in those instances when you've been hurt. Pray for those who have hurt you and for patience with them.

2. Ask for God's help in those areas where you need more patience.

For Homework:

List three areas where you need more patience. Alongside each one, write out a scripture that can help you (from this chapter or elsewhere).
    1)

2)

3)

2. Read the following scriptures and list the ways Jesus showed patience:
Mark 2:1-36:

John 6:1-14:

Chapter Ten

The Garment of Joy

"You turned my wailing into dancing; you removed my sackcloth and clothed me with joy, that my heart may sing your praises and not be silent. Lord my God, I will praise you forever." (Psalm 30:11-12 NIV)

If you were to see someone in the Garment of Joy, they would be wearing a bright floral print dress. Just as this kind of clothing brightens up a room, the spiritual Garment of Joy brings streams of sunshine. True joy lifts our countenance and gives us strength to be a blessing to everyone around us. It certainly cheers us more than a drab sackcloth tunic of despair.

What makes *you* so happy you want to sing? Is it your new home, your tropical vacation, your kids, your boyfriend, your husband, your career, your car? Or is it Jesus? The Lord wants to be the joy of your heart, and He created you with the longing and capacity to know Him in that way. What you taste, feel, smell, hear, and see distracts from that spiritual reality because you want immediate gratification. Other things make you happy for a while, but they don't satisfy your spirit. Anything except Jesus eventually disappoints, grows dull, or gets broken. Only He satisfies the deep need of your heart—that need for love and contentment.

When Jesus is the source of our joy, our view of other things changes. It's not that temporal things are evil—they have their place; in fact, they're for our enjoyment. When we see our blessings from God as a testimony of His love, we enjoy them more. We look at blooming flowers as God's art, and we worship Him for His masterful creation. We enjoy our children as God's borrowed angels (or rascals) to love and care for. We view our husbands with a deeper, giving love drawn from God's agape storehouse. We can be thankful for all of God's goodness, knowing it's given for our pleasure.

When we find our joy in the Lord, He promises our heart's desire, fruitfulness, and blessing. I pray that we would focus our attention on Him because He is so good to delight in. We could praise Him forever and still not measure His greatness. The following verses speak about making Him our delight:

"Delight yourself also in the Lord, and He shall give you the desires of your heart" (Psalm 37:4).

"Blessed (or happy) is the man who walks not in the counsel of the ungodly, nor stands in the path of sinners, nor sits in the seat of the scornful; but his delight is in the law of the Lord, and in His law, he meditates day and night. He shall be like a tree planted by the rivers of water, that brings forth its fruit in its season, whose leaf also shall not wither; and whatever he does shall prosper" (Psalm 1:1-3).

Meditate on God's word day and night, as you drive down the road during the day and as you lay in bed at night. Let His promises and counsel fill your mind. The emotion of happiness will come and go as circumstances change, but joy is the emotion of great delight caused by something good or satisfying.

God, in His love, wants us to be content and joyful people because He is so satisfying. As we realize His love for us and walk with Him daily, we can know true joy that doesn't go away, even when bad things happen.

So Many Reasons

"In Your presence is fullness of joy" (Psalm 16:11).

Do you know that the God of the entire universe is **with us**? In fact, one of the Lord's names, *Emmanuel*, means "God with us." He is a friend who's constantly present and wants to help us with everything we're going through. Who wouldn't want a friend like that? He shows Himself strong in our lives when we wait on Him and believe His promises—and there's a wealth of them. Hold on to His promises, and let Him prove that He's true to His word. He wants to give us joy in our walk. May we become more aware of this truth, living in fellowship with our Lord, as the beloved hymn "What a Friend We Have in Jesus" declares.

God promises to bring **joy from sorrow**. Psalm 126 and Isaiah 51:11 both describe how the Israelites felt sorrowful when they returned from captivity in Babylon. At times, we can relate to their sorrow because we experience our own forms of captivity caused by sin. We mourn over the effects of past sins and grieve over the consequences of our unfaithfulness to God. We also sorrow over current heartaches, losses, and broken relationships. It is a good thing to grieve over our pain and follow the natural progression through loss. But God promises to bring joy through these experiences and give hope that we will smile again. He will work all things together for good (Rom. 8:28). Know that whatever you're facing has a divine purpose for your highest good. Sorrow can prepare us for joy, and even enlarge our capacity for it. Hold on to God's promises and acknowledge His sovereignty. You will know joy again.

In chapter 2 we learned about the **joy we have from our salvation.** It's exciting to realize we have a relationship with Jesus, and to know that soon we will be His bride. We are also joyful because of the completed work of our salvation. We can rest completely in Him and His righteousness, and we can respond by living in thanksgiving and praise. To read more about this joy, see Psalm 51:12, Isaiah 61:10, Psalm 21:1, and Psalm 13:5.

The writer of Psalm 89:16 said, "In Your name they rejoice all day long." Even more than sweethearts doodling each other's names, we can have joy in our relationship with our incredible Savior.

We're commanded to be **joyful at the blessings of God.** In Deuteronomy 16:15, the Israelites celebrated a week-long feast to acknowledge the Lord's provision because He provided it for their joy. You would think this celebration would have been easy. But how many times do we forget that the blessings from God are for our enjoyment? We often take them for granted or chock them up to chance. Psalm 105 tells us to remember all the deeds He does and tell others about them (like celebrating Thanksgiving several times a year, especially the pumpkin pie part!).

Joy is a fruit of the Holy Spirit, Galatians 5:22: When we're living in the control, power, and direction of the Holy Spirit, joy is a natural quality. Fruit trees don't strain to bear fruit; it grows naturally. Are you experiencing this supernatural and delicious joy?

Persecution for Christ's sake leads to joy, Matthew 5:11-12 and Acts 5:4: If people hate us because we follow Christ and live according to His principles, we know we're doing something right. We also know the enemy doesn't like it. After all, Jesus Himself was persecuted. "Yes, and all who desire to live godly in Christ Jesus will suffer persecution," II Timothy 3:12 says. That's a promise we don't like to claim, but it ultimately leads to joy.

We may not see many martyrs in the US these days, but have you ever been treated poorly at work for not lying about something? Persecution has less obvious ways of showing itself. In Acts 5:41, after Peter and the apostles were persecuted by the religious leaders, they rejoiced because they had been considered worthy to suffer for the Lord's name. They considered it an honor, perhaps knowing they were like Him in a small way, and remembering His promise of heavenly blessing. God's ways are not our ways, and this concept may be hard to understand. But His promise of joy is the result.

Faith leads to joy, Romans 15:13 and Philippians 1:25: Faith is believing in God's goodness when we can't see the answer. Having joy from our faith goes beyond the patience of faith from chapter 9. We can experience the joyful expectation of a promise fulfilled without knowing the answer yet. I'm waiting on God in several areas of my life, and I feel peace and assurance that He will answer. If what I have is true faith, there's a certain amount of joy in the waiting because I know He will be true to His promises to my family and to me. We can have this joyful faith in Him for every detail of our lives. In the big picture, our faith in Christ leads to joy, knowing we will be with Him someday in a perfect place.

Hope leads to joy, Romans 5:2 and Romans 12:12: Hope is the anchor of our faith, and without it we lose heart. Hope connects our faith to its desired outcome. Knowing our hope is in God, we believe He only allows what's best for us because in the end, He will right all wrongs. Hope gives us vision for better things and trust that He will meet all our needs. Dare to hope that God wants to do great things through you, and be excited about it!

We can share in the joy of others. We can truly be joyful for the good fortune of others instead of concealing jealousy and faking happiness We can do this by living that adage: **J**esus first, **O**thers second, and **Y**ourself last equals Joy! "Rejoice with those who rejoice" (Rom 12:15).

These are all great promises, but how do we practice them in real life? Prayer is the best place to start. Take your sorrows to Him, and He will bring the comfort you need. When you look to Jesus, He gives you the strength, encouragement, and patience to hold on for the answer. Whatever your loss, He wants to make up what's lacking. Read the Scriptures to find your daily spiritual nourishment. He will speak to you, and when He does, it will bring joy. Know that God made you lovingly, and He wants to speak into every area of your life.

Sarcasm and cynicism kill true joy. Finding humor in the failings of others is arrogant and not the way Jesus responds. But viewing everything with naivety isn't right either. Maturity allows us to see the truth yet respond with love and patience. Sarcasm is popular in the intellectual crowd. It's easy to put others down to get a laugh— laughing with friends is a highlight of life. Yet this is the wrong avenue to joy. If you've been the brunt of a joke, you know how much it hurts and how unloving it feels.

So many people are unhappy. You can see in their eyes that they're walking zombies, stuck in their painful lives. Yes, life is hard and sometimes hellish. But as we remember all the promises of God— that He is with us always, He works all things for good, and He loves us with an everlasting love—we can live differently. He fills us with His life and that means a creative, ever-renewing, joyful existence.

Do you experience creativity in your daily life? Do you see beauty in the blessings He's given? That's a reason for joy! He has set us free from the law of sin and death. We have hope! We don't have to be bogged down with the drudgery around us. Depression can leave us feeling hopeless—I know, I've been there. My comfy bed looks so good some days. But the way out of hopelessness is to "arise and shine" and to obey God, one step at a time. If you believe in Him, then get up and walk in Him. As you take a little step, He will meet you with strength for the journey.

There are so many ways the Lord wants to bring us joy. We have a reason to wear the Garment of Joy with confidence. His joy is not a phony mask, but a real faith-inspired, deep-rooted, trusting smile— as obvious as a brightly colored dress.

For Discussion:

1. What's the difference between happiness and joy?

2. Are there any situations when joy would be impossible? Explain.

3. Have you ever been persecuted? What happened?

4. If you answered yes to #3, did you experience joy? If yes, how?

5. Describe someone you know who wears the Garment of Joy. What is he or she like?

For Prayer:

1. Take your burdens to the Lord in prayer. Wait on Him to give you the faith to believe in His goodness for you.

2. Pray that you will be a blessing to others through the joy He's promised to clothe you in.

For Homework and Application:

Share about a time when the Lord turned your sorrow into joy.

Chapter Eleven

Garment of Power

"I am going to send you what My Father has promised; but stay in the city until you have been clothed with power from on high."
(Luke 24:49 NIV)

The power Jesus promised to clothe His disciples with was the person of the Holy Spirit. We might picture this Garment of Power as a workout suit. With the Holy Spirit in our lives, we have the power to overcome sin, to love unlovable people, and to change the world with the gospel of Jesus. Wow, He's given us some muscle! As we do these things, we exercise or practice all the things we've learned. The Lord Himself dons you with the Garment of Power. Let's look at what being clothed with His power means.

Every believer receives the Holy Spirit when he or she is born again. This is what Jesus referred to in John 3:5-8 when He said that everyone who wants eternal life must be born of the Spirit. In Luke 24:49, however, Jesus talked about the *baptism* of the Holy Spirit, which is different. The first time this baptism happened was in the second chapter of Acts.

The First Fill-Up (Full Service, Not Self-Serve)

The gifts and the fruit of the Spirit accompanied this first filling, when the gift of tongues and other gifts were given. In Acts 2:14, Peter delivered a powerful sermon, even though before that time he had denied the Lord and gone into hiding. But after Pentecost the Holy Spirit gave incredible gifts of teaching, exhortation, and evangelism. This resulted in three thousand believers being added to the church in one day! Verse 41 describes these new believers and how the Holy Spirit transformed them. As they shared their possessions, they operated in the gift of giving, and signs and wonders also took place among them. Their assemblies were characterized by joy, truth, praise, fellowship, and prayer.

Refills

We see many other examples of the Holy Spirit's work throughout the book of Acts. In Acts 4:3 after the believers were filled with the Spirit, they began speaking the Word of God boldly. In the story of Ananias and Sapphira in Acts 5:1-11, we see the Holy Spirit's intolerance for sin. The Gentiles speak in tongues and praise God after receiving the Spirit in Acts 10:46. And in Acts 13:52, the disciples were continually filled with joy and the Holy Spirit.

Believers received the filling, or baptism, on the day of Pentecost, and they experienced other fillings after that. In Ephesians 5:18 the Apostle Paul tells believers to "be filled with the Spirit." This word *be* means to "be being filled." Two different things are happening here—the initial filling, or the baptism, and then subsequent fillings—like fresh water poured into an empty cup. In ministry, the Holy Spirit is the living water as described by Jesus in John 4:10, poured out in a believer's life, and that water needs to be refreshed and refilled.

The Holy Spirit is a person who lives inside of us, and we're filled and refilled by coming to Him and asking. He wants to have a relationship with us, but a one-time encounter is not a meaningful relationship. Our relationship with the Lord, through His Spirit, should be a daily, living, communicating friendship.

Gifts for All

When we receive Christ as our Savior, we receive the Holy Spirit. Then we should pray to be filled, or baptized, with the Holy Spirit as well. Wait on the Lord, and He will do this for you. When you are filled with the Spirit, you will receive one or more of His gifts for ministry to the church. If you already know what your gifts are, you need to ask the Lord for a refilling often so you can continue to minister the fresh, living water of His Spirit. We learn in I Corinthians 13 that the purpose of the gifts is love, and without love, the gifts are useless. They are not given for ourselves but to serve God and others.

The fruit of the Spirit should be evident in every believer. "But the fruit of the Spirit is love, joy, peace, longsuffering, kindness, goodness, faithfulness, gentleness, self-control. Against such there is no law" (Galatians 5:22-23). These fruits should also be evident in the way a gift of the Spirit is used. For example, if a believer has the gift of exhortation—which is correcting a person who is in error—love should be communicated above all. If the person receiving correction goes away feeling cared for, knowing God wants them to stop a harmful behavior for their good, then this gift was truly used in love. If the person goes away feeling like they received a condescending, condemning lecture, then the fruit of that gift could have been rotten. Not every rebuke is received, even when it's given in love. However, if it is well received, then it was probably given in a loving way.

Being clothed with power means that we have the Lord's strength to overcome sin. This is the most miraculous show of the His power in our lives. Without Him, humanity is on a path toward self-destruction. Yet His power enables us to choose life and righteousness in our decisions.

Much controversy exists about the Holy Spirit in the church today. Some believe the gifts were done away with after Pentecost, and others say that the Lord added more gifts later, including dog barking and laughing in the Spirit. Yet spiritual gifts are not meant to be frightening, controversial, or centered on man's ego.

The gifts are for today because the perfect kingdom has not yet come (I Cor. 13:9-10). We need the ministry of the Spirit in our church and fellowship groups—this is the way the Lord shows Himself and reveals His power. Every gift has a vital place in the church today. Good teaching is inspired by the Holy Spirit. Giving benefits the needy. And mercy ministers to hurting sinners.

Just as each part of our physical body has a different function, each member of Christ's body has a unique role. The eye sees and the ear hears, and we'd be in trouble if they traded places. It's inspiring to see the different gifts in the church and how they're shared. My husband and I are one example of these differences. We write music together, and we often clash about how the direction of a song should go. His writing gift expresses exhortation and truth-telling, and I write lyrics about grace and mercy. We balance each other out! Since Jesus was full of grace *and* truth (John 1:14), both are needed in the body, working together to present a balanced picture of Him. We're *all* needed in the body of Christ, and we can't exist independently of each other.

I challenge you to seek the Lord for the spiritual gifts He's given you. If you desire a specific gift, begin praying for it. Spend time waiting on Him—He wants to clothe you with power and make you useful. Whether it's your first time to be filled with the Holy Spirit or you need a re-filling, grow strong in Him and in His power.

The following are lists all the spiritual gifts and where they're found in the New Testament:

Romans 12:6-8 – Prophecy, service, teaching, exhortation, giving, leading and mercy.

I Corinthians 12:8-10 – Word of wisdom, word of knowledge, faith, miracles, prophecy, discerning spirits, tongues, interpretation of tongues.

I Corinthians 12:28 – Apostles, prophets, teachers, miracles, healing, helps, administration, tongues.

Ephesians 4:11 – Apostles, prophets, evangelists, pastors, teachers.

The Holy Spirit challenges you to *experience* the Christian life, not just know about it. He wants you to truly share the luscious taste of His sweet fruit, operate in the unique gifts He has for you, and know His strength of victory over sin. It's time to suit up with the Garment of Power and head to the gym of life!

For Discussion:

1. Do you have any areas of confusion about the gifts of the Holy Spirit? If yes, explain.

2. How has the Holy Spirit made a difference in your life?

3. Give an example of how the gifts and the fruit of the Spirit operate in harmony.

For Prayer:

Seek the Lord regarding your part in the body of Christ, and pray for opportunities to use your gifts for His glory this week (Rom. 12:6-8, I Cor. 12:8-10, I Cor. 12:28, and Eph. 4:11).

For Homework and Application:

List your spiritual gifts. Explain why you think the Lord has given you these, and share one example of how He has used this gifting in you.

Chapter Twelve

Shoes of Forgiveness

"Forgive us our sins as we have forgiven those who sin against us."
(Matthew 6:12 NLT)

After we are saved, we are later bathed—in a spiritual sense. In other words, our feet get dirty as we travel life's path, and we need to be washed. In John 13:3-17, Jesus showed Himself to be a servant when He washed His disciples' feet and then told them to do the same. Like Jesus, we wash one another's feet, symbolically, whenever we forgive each other.

We all must learn how to forgive. There are moments when I think I'm pretty good at it. It's easy to forgive a small matter—I can usually brush it off and say, "People are people!" But it's a lot harder to forgive when I'm deeply hurt. If someone steals something, damages my reputation, or even wounds my pride, forgiveness may feel excruciating.

Still, Jesus tells us to wash each other's feet. As we grow together in the body of Christ, we're bound to hurt one another along the way. None of us are perfect. And so, we must learn to forgive.

Think of the Shoes of Forgiveness as clear glass slippers. Perhaps the mention of glass slippers brings Cinderella to mind. Imagine this character for a moment and consider a few things about her. How did she remain beautiful and full of grace when she was bombarded with harsh words and commands? Though forgiveness wasn't the theme of Cinderella's story, in real life we know that a person couldn't keep submitting to their tormenters without a heart of forgiveness and love. Glass slippers were the perfect finishing touch for Cinderella's gown because the purity of forgiveness was part of her character.

What if Cinderella had worn mud-caked hiking boots with her elegant gown? Filthy boots would have spoiled her ensemble, just like unforgiveness can spoil our spiritual beauty. The sin of bitterness, if it takes root in our heart, will grow and grow until it's sprouting right out of our mouth!

We all know we're *supposed* to forgive, but how do we do it? As with the other spiritual garments, it's impossible to wear the Shoes of Forgiveness without the Lord's help. First, we need to take our situation to Him and ask for His help. Next, we need to ask for His help and lastly, we need His help! Get the point? When we're terribly hurt, it may take years to process and be completely free. But the Lord wants us to allow Him to take us through it.

One difficult aspect of forgiveness is the pain we feel while forgiveness is happening. The person who forgives must bear the pain of whatever has taken place. Naturally, we try to avoid pain, so the concept of willingly bearing it may seem foreign. But if we let the affliction caused by someone else have its work in us, knowing God may be allowing it for our maturity, we will benefit, because God will ultimately work His forgiveness in our heart.

Remember the story of Joseph's reunion with his brothers in Egypt? The brothers were afraid to face Joseph after the horrible way they'd treated him years before. But Joseph told them, "You meant evil against me, but God meant it for good." (Gen. 50:20). Perhaps Joseph had to work on forgiving his brothers during those long years in an Egyptian prison. And while his example is admirable, consider our supreme example, Jesus, who bore more pain than any human could experience when he hung on the cross and forgave all the sins of mankind.

It's good to pray about your feelings as you seek to forgive. Psalm 62:8 says to "pour out your heart before Him." You don't have to wait until your heart and mind are uncluttered before talking to Him. He wants to hear *everything*—heartache and all. As you pray, search your Bible for His words to you. Spend time being still and knowing that He is God (Psalm 46:10). He will bring the word of hope you need.

When we're offended, revenge may be crouching at the door. Beware of this response, in all its insidious forms, because without God's supernatural help, our flesh *will* take revenge. That's why there are so many verses about letting God fight for us. We need to be reminded of this because it's tempting to talk about whoever has hurt us to justify ourselves and find pity. However, it's better to seek out godly people who are removed from the situation and can help us process through the pain. Let's avoid explaining and defending ourselves and remember that God will take care of us. He will remember our cause and will bring all things to light in the end.

As we travel through life, it's inevitable that we'll get hurt, experience pain, and need to forgive others. Wearing the Shoes of Forgiveness can get us to the end of the road graciously. Not only will we be dressed in a stunning robe of righteousness with jewels, we'll also have a perfect pair of shoes to match.

For Discussion:

1. Hebrews 12:15 says, "Looking carefully lest anyone fall short of the grace of God; lest any root of bitterness springing up cause trouble, and by this many become defiled."
   How is bitterness manifested or seen in a person?

2. List three practical ways you can show forgiveness to people in your life:
1)
2)
3)

3. Describe someone you know, someone like Cinderella, who has remained kind and beautiful, even through difficult circumstances

For Prayer:

1. Pray about any unforgiveness you may be holding in your heart. Confess your need for the Lord's help to let go of it.

2. Pray for those who have hurt you and for those you may have hurt. Prayer is important in the process of forgiveness, both for you and for the other person.

For Homework:

1. Memorize Ephesians 4:32: "Be kind to one another, tenderhearted, forgiving one another, even as God in Christ forgave you."

2. Read the parable of the unmerciful servant in Matthew 18:21-35. Write down your thoughts about how much the Lord has forgiven you. Spend time in His presence, thanking Him for the gift of eternal life you have because of His forgiveness.

Chapter Thirteen

Garment of Strength and Dignity

"Strength and dignity are her clothing, and she smiles at the future."
(Prov. 31:25 NASB)

Proverbs 31 describes the amazing virtuous woman. Sometimes this woman seems almost *too* amazing to be real. She manages to take care of her family, her household, her business, and herself—in addition to doing community service! We read in verse 25 that she's clothed with "strength and dignity" (NASB).

Picture this woman in a stunning business suit. Dressed in the Garment of Strength and Dignity, she exudes confidence, security, and self-control. Without being domineering or pushy, she handles affairs at home and out in the world with a solid trust in the Lord. Because *He* is her confidence, she isn't ensnared by the fear of man or the enemy. She's secure in God's love, and she knows that whatever He has for her to do, He will provide all she needs.

Strength

The word *strength* has many meanings, including ability, firmness, alertness, energy, fortitude, glory, sincerity, and truth. Strength also means to hold fast, to make firm, to have completeness, to be pure and solid like gold, and to uphold, support, and protect. Finally, spiritual strength means to have the might and power of God!

As Christian women, we want to be strong in the Lord, not in ourselves. When our strength runs out, He wants us to rely on Him. Godly strength differs from the world's idea of strength. For example, a successful businesswoman in the world's view may be controlling and manipulative. Her strength is measured in how many people she uses, outsmarts, or steps on to get where she is.

My husband exemplifies a successful businessman who maintains his integrity as a believer. He seeks to serve his clients and meet their needs instead of simply making big bucks. Though others around him lie and use devious methods of getting business, he tells the truth. Because of his honesty, he's earned the highest respect of other associates in his field. Dignity and strength—the garment worn by the Proverbs 31 woman—is characterized by truth and love. In Psalm 73:25-28, Asaph, a leader in David's choir, acknowledged his desperate need for strength:

"Whom have I in heaven but You? And there is none upon earth that I desire besides You. My flesh and my heart fail; but God is the strength of my heart and my portion forever. For indeed, those who are far from You shall perish; You have destroyed all those who desert You for harlotry. But it is good for me to draw near to God; I have put my trust in the Lord God, that I may declare all Your works."

We need to fall on the Lord's strength for every situation in life. Yet we seldom realize the depth of our weakness because we're so self-sufficient. When we truly believe God will never abandon us, we can completely rely on Him to bring the help we need. We can let go of our self-strength and trust Him to do what needs to be done. In our weakness, He is strong (II Cor. 12:9), and this principle is the basis of our faith. What should you do when you're in an overwhelming situation? Take it to the Lord. He will either help you through it step by step or provide a way out (I Cor. 10:13). This is true not only for temptation, but also for any challenges you face.

Ability

Proverbs 22:29 says, "Do you see a man who excels in his work? He will stand before kings; He will not stand before unknown men." Be good at what you do for His glory. The Lord wants you to use what you're given and to invest your time and talents wisely (Matt. 25:14-30).

We're accountable to God for what we're given. Will we bury our talents out of fear? Or will we be faithful to do our best for Him with what He entrusts to us? Just like learning to play the piano, practicing and working hard is the only way to become proficient. This includes the way we serve in our home, our church, and our job.

Tell the Truth

Additional aspects of strength include truth and sincerity. God created you to be exactly who you are. If He calls you to be a leader and you aren't a strong one naturally, you don't have to fake it. Instead of acting like you think a leader should act, let God use your honesty. He wants to make you strong in Him. Timothy was young when he was called into ministry, and he had major responsibilities early on. Paul wrote two epistles to him, which include this encouragement from II Timothy 1:7: "For God has not given us a spirit of fear, but of power and of love and of a sound mind." When we feel weak, it's a *good* thing because that's when God shows the strength of His Spirit in us.

Complete and Lacking Nothing

Completeness is also a strength. The virtuous woman of Proverbs 31 had it all together (I can't picture her as only half-together). The Lord wants to help us with our schedules, which in God's scheme of things may seem insignificant to us. Yet He can be trusted to guide us in managing our time and getting things done. He's interested in our day-to-day lives.

A complete person isn't needy and doesn't depend on others in unhealthy ways. She stays focused throughout her day, even when she doesn't have support or encouragement from others. And though the Proverbs 31 woman is married, she clearly has the wisdom to make business decisions on her own (verses 16,18, and 24).

Sometimes it's easy to neglect certain tasks that need attention at home or work and leave them for someone else, like our husband. But when possible, try to take the initiative to help with these jobs, even if they're not yours to do. It will be appreciated.

Experiencing an intense, exhilarating physical workout gives you the feeling that you can conquer anything. In the same way, experiencing this spiritual aspect of strength gives you confidence that God will help you through whatever comes. Combined with dignity, being complete and lacking nothing in Him is an attractive spiritual attribute.

The Dignified One

Dignity means elegance, greatness, majesty, nobility, high condition, and elevation of character. It means to be formal in conduct and speech, and completely respectable. When I hear the word *dignitary*, I think of world leaders, the Royal Family, and princes and princesses. These dignitaries are imperfect like the rest of us but thankfully, true dignity is unlike what we see modeled by the world. For believers, dignity means that we have the Lord's goodness in our lives. Because we are now His children, we are royalty as sons and daughters of the King. This knowledge shouldn't make us proud or haughty but should give us reason to stand tall, with security and confidence.

Classy Lady

What kind of first impression do you leave? A person with dignity has class. Do others view you this way? In Proverbs 31:25, the dignity of the virtuous woman is such a vital part of her character that it's noticed as much as her clothing.

Remember, it's not classy to dress trashy. Sexualizing our appearance in public may bring momentary attention, but ultimately it brings disrespect. When women put it all out there, they lower the respect level for *all* women. We're not created to be objects for man's entertainment. Sex in marriage is the place for mutual loving expression. Wearing dignity means bringing Christ's love and grace to others. Reserve your sexy for your husband.

In the Light

Having dignity also means living in such a way that you never need to be ashamed of anything you do, say, or create. It means never cutting corners and never having reason to hide or blush about your behavior. The Bible tells us to live in the light (John 12:35-36 and 46, and I John 1:7). The way to do this is to abide in the Lord, believe Him, and let every action be filtered through the question: Would this please Him? Consider Jesus' example and ask yourself, "How would He handle this situation?" He is right beside you and will give you the strength to walk in dignity.

A woman clothed in strength and dignity is radiant. She's strong in God's goodness, not in herself. She smiles at the future. She looks everyone in the eye and speaks resolutely with strength. She does excellent work. She doesn't have skeletons in her closet, and she makes amends with anyone she hurts along the way. With nothing to fear, she's secure in the knowledge that the Lord is with her in every situation. The strength and dignity of a woman is a significant part of her beauty.

For Discussion:

1. How can the Lord be our strength in a practical way?
2. List two ways you can show dignity in your life:
   1)
   2)

3. Describe an elegant woman you know. Why do you think she is that way?

4. Why is a woman clothed with strength and dignity able to smile at the future?

For Prayer:

1. Pray that you would know the Lord's strength, specifically in areas where you feel weak.

2. Pray about any areas in your life that need dignity. Repent of anything you are ashamed of, and ask for God's help to walk in His light.

For Homework and Application:

1. Read Psalm 73:25-28. Describe a time in your life when God was your strength and how His nearness was your good.

2. Identify three areas where you need His strength now:
   1)
   2)
   3)

3. Write down a talent you feel the Lord may want you to develop further. Ask for His guidance in this and for opportunities to use it for His glory.

Chapter Fourteen

Garment of Fine Linen and Purple

"Her clothing is fine linen and purple." (Prov. 31:22)

Not only did the incredible Proverbs 31 woman take care of her family, household, and business, she also took care of herself. This gem of a woman was clothed in "fine linen and purple" (verse 22), which in her culture was the most fashionable clothing available. Attention to appearance was a detail she minded well. Some of us prefer the sweats and hair scrunchie look, but this is quite unlike our Bible grandmother's example.

Linen was typically worn only by kings, priests, and others of high rank. In the same way, we value high thread count linens today, so it was in Bible times—the finer the weave, the more valuable the cloth. Purple cloth was similarly sought after. Although an assortment of dyes wasn't available, dyes from natural sources were used, and a good purple color was hard to obtain. Purple came from making liquor out of a shellfish called the pinna magna, or sea hedgehog as it's called today, which is found in the Mediterranean Sea.

The story of Lydia from Philippi in Acts 16:13-15 tells us that she was a seller of purple cloth. Evidently, people were trained professionally in this occupation, and the exact method was so secret that the art was lost with that civilization. Wearing fine linen and purple was considered extraordinary. The Proverbs 31 woman *was* extraordinary, adorning herself with a lovely purple fine linen gown. Because this detail of clothing was included as one of the Proverbs 31 woman's attributes, it's worth pondering.

Unlike the other garments we've looked at, this one has to do with outward appearance. Some believe that looking beautiful is unspiritual, and certainly an obsession with our appearance is unwise. I Peter 3:3-4 says," Do not let your adornment be merely outward—arranging the hair, wearing gold, or putting on fine apparel—rather let it be the hidden person of the heart, with the incorruptible beauty of a gentle and quiet spirit, which is very precious in the sight of God."

Certain cults and religious groups leave out the word *merely* and set up legalistic requirements for their women, like wearing only black or using no make-up. There is a balance. True beauty comes from within; that is, Jesus in our hearts and His character manifesting itself through us (as in the qualities we've studied). Yet, God created our physical beauty to be enjoyed. There is nothing wrong with wanting to look our best with the resources we have.

Religious extremism isn't the only thing that affects our views about beauty. For example, Patty was an attractive college girl who loved dressing up for dates with her boyfriend. She looked great in stylish dresses and jean jackets, with her hair done up as big as Texas. She found her man and her ring, and a few years later the babies started coming. With each birth, she gave up a little more in the looks department until no one could mistake her profession as a full-time mom. Given that she felt too tired to care, she was fine with wearing baggy sweats and oversized T-shirts almost every day. Besides, she saw this attire modeled by her own Mom. After a while, her husband missed the cute, spunky Patty he'd fallen in love with, and it became increasingly difficult for him to refuse advances from the attractive women at work.

Amanda was considered the cool girl in the singles group, with lots of guy pals. With a fit, athletic build, she had an aversion to looking too feminine. Dressing up wasn't her style—it made her uncomfortable. Whenever the guys talked sports stats, she fit right in, preferring their conversation over women's chitchat. She often had secret crushes on her guy friends, hoping they'd return her affection, but they never did. She managed fine as a single woman but felt sad that she'd never had a family of her own.

Kelly's parents had marital problems. They were professing Christians and even took their family to church, but several times Kelly had walked in on her dad while he was viewing pornography at home. Meanwhile, Kelly's mom went through a phase of wearing low-cut tops and tight pants. Then one day they all found out that Dad was having an affair, and suddenly the marriage ended. In the aftermath, Kelly was left alone to sort out what it meant to be a Christian woman. She felt driven by the strong need to wear the latest fashions, especially sexy clothes. She worked hard to have a toned figure, and she exercised incessantly alongside a personal trainer. With platinum-dyed hair, tanned skin year-round, and fake nails and eyelashes, Kelly always looked perfect.

Patty, Amanda, and Kelly all need healing in their view of outward beauty. Patty needs to know that she still shines and has her own unique beauty. Many women find it easier to let their mom persona overshadow everything else. Sometimes that pretty woman with a sexy side for her husband is gradually forgotten, but in a healthy marriage that element should continue. Kids benefit from seeing their parents in love with each other. Children grow up and couples are eventually alone again. Sadly, many divorces occur at this point, even after 30 years of marriage. As wives, it's important to make the effort to be attractive for our husbands.

"But my husband should love me just the way I am," you say. But really, only God can do that. I Samuel 16:7 teaches that 'man looks at the outward appearance, but the Lord looks at the heart.'" We all desire to be loved unconditionally, the way God loves us with His *agape* love. *Agape,* a Greek word, describes God's undeserved, sacrificing, incomparable love for humankind.

God's love is complete and constant. We see glimpses of agape love in human relationships, but they're only glimpses. We're all temporal and needy, and we *still* look on the outside. Any loving relationship requires effort. If one person is the only giver, forgiver, or server, this puts a heavy strain on the relationship. As humans, we're weak. Perfection should not be required, but a little effort toward appearance goes a long way.

What about Amanda? There's nothing wrong with a sporty style and a good rapport with guy friends. But if those tendencies stem from a missing dad or some other childhood issue, this should be prayed through and possibly some Bible-based counseling would be helpful.

You are designed uniquely by your heavenly Father, and He loves you! You are His princess. He's created you with an inward desire to be loved by Him, by your family, and then—unless you are called to a life of singleness—by a man. Most men love women who are comfortable with their femininity.

An overemphasis on the external can get out of balance, as in Kelly's story. Kelly looks for approval through outward perfection. And what happens when she runs out of the money it takes to maintain her muscle tone, hair color, tan, nails, and eyelashes? Does her world fall apart? As Christian women, our answer is to seek God for our stability because He is the lover of our souls. Kelly needs to look to Him, and to caring women who can guide her into the Lord's love for her. Then she'll be attractive in the truest sense, and her outward beauty will be in balance.

Physical appearance reflects what's in your heart. What do you reflect? Are you the lovely, giving woman God created you to be, wearing the character traits we've talked about so far? Or do you reflect fear, laziness, immorality, or insecurity?

We all need to pay some attention to wearing the fine linen and purple, or being the best we can be, like the Proverbs 31 woman. Looking our best is a godly trait. In healthy relationships, no one expects perfection, but making an effort to look good on the outside is a part of living out beauty in action as a godly woman.

A Healthy You

Take an inventory of your health. If you feel good, you look good. Are you doing what you should to maintain your well-being? Do you eat a healthy diet, exercise regularly, sleep well, and deal with stress positively? Do you have any harmful habits such as smoking, drinking too much, drug use, overeating, or under-eating? God wants to help you with any of these unhealthy behaviors.

Get Stress Free

How do we live stress free? Ha! There's no way to completely avoid stress—we can only change the way we deal with it. Proverbs 17:22 tells us, "A merry heart does good, like medicine." While I was pregnant with my first child, my OB-GYN doctor counseled me to be happy throughout my pregnancy. She told all her patients to watch funny movies, stay away from depressing friends, and avoid stressful situations. After years of dispensing this advice, she found that the health of her patients and their babies benefited. According to HelpGuide.org, studies show that laughter releases stress-fighting chemicals that improve health (see **www.helpguide.org/articles/emotional-health/laughter-is-the-best-medicine.htm**). Once again, science came up with something God had already thought of. Laugh for the health of it!

Philippians 4:6 says, "Be anxious for nothing, but in everything by prayer and supplication, with thanksgiving, let your requests be known to God."
Most women I know worry naturally. We typically want to talk about a problem before—or instead of—praying. We like to process and receive sympathy from each other, and some of this is fine. But if we would only prove the reality of this verse, we'd experience so much more peace. How can we let go of our concerns? Philippians 4:7-9 offers this advice:

"And the peace of God, which surpasses all understanding, will guard your hearts and minds through Christ Jesus. Finally, brethren, whatever things are true, whatever things are noble, whatever things are just, whatever things are pure, whatever things are lovely, whatever things are of good report, if there is any virtue and if there is anything praiseworthy—meditate on these things. The things which you learned and received and heard and saw in me, these do, and the God of peace will be with you."

Let's pray for our concerns with an attitude of thanksgiving. When we feel the urge to worry, let's think about what is true and noble and just. Most of our worries are about the "what ifs," yet God promises, as we see in the passage above, to be the God of peace to us. It may be difficult to let go when we want control, but we must remember that He can handle everything.

How content *are* you? Paul shares his view on contentment in Philippians 4:11b-12: "For I have learned in whatever state I am, to be content: I know how to be abased, and I know how to abound. Everywhere and in all things, I have learned both to be full and to be hungry, both to abound and to suffer need."

When we're frustrated, many of us take on a critical perspective. But like Paul, we need to learn contentment. Often, we live in a state of expectation for the future, imagining that everything will be perfect someday, but this is unrealistic. The person who has learned contentment truly shines for the Lord and lives out a deep trust in His care. We can choose our attitude, and it's time to choose contentment.

Actress Marilyn Monroe said: "A smile is the best make-up a girl could wear." Her quote reminds me of the yellow smiley face icon that became popular in the 70s, long before emoticons. Though I loved this little yellow friend, some people thought it signified a brainless, shallow person, perhaps because there was no apparent reason for his cheery grin. If we scan the faces in a crowd, we'll see many who look grumpy or depressed, and they probably are. But for those who are truly living out their faith, there's a reason for the joy reflected on their faces. A simple smile can change someone's day— or the atmosphere of an entire room. Even if we put on a smile by faith, and we arise and shine out of obedience, we'll be encouraged and changed.

A poll taken by FamilyShare.com revealed that one of a husband's favorite things to see is his wife's smile (**www.familyshare.com/marriage/12-signs-your-wife-is-happily-married**). And according to songwriters Nichols, Giles, and Godard, "When Momma ain't happy, ain't nobody happy" ("When Mama Ain't Happy". EMI Music Publishing; Warner/Chappell Music, Inc.; Universal Publishing Group, 1998).

If something so simple as a smile can make a man feel like he's on top of the world, why don't we do it more often? Is it so hard to look at life in a positive light and be thankful for the good things? Do we have to obsess and feel sad until every circumstance lines up perfectly to our dreams?

American novelist Kurt Vonnegut once said, "Enjoy the little things in life for one day you'll look back and realize they were the big things." Just smile!

Weight affects our appearance, and many of us find it extremely hard to manage. As Christian women, we don't do drugs or party, so what else do we have? Eating may be one of our only pleasures. However, God asks us to be a good steward of what He's given, and this includes our body. Overeating and under-eating can damage our health, relationships, and appearance. Turning to the latest fad diet isn't the answer either; it will ultimately take us backwards.

If you're concerned about body image or if you feel in bondage to food, seek God. Ask Him how He wants to deliver you. The way we eat is ingrained in us, and we need the Lord's help and the support of others to change. Many excellent Bible studies and support groups can offer assistance. Two popular Bible-based weight control programs are *Made to Crave: Satisfying Your Deepest Desire with God, Not Food* by Lysa TerKeurst (Zondervan 2010) and *The Daniel Plan: 40 Days to a Healthier Life* by Pastor Rick Warren, Dr. Daniel Amen, and Dr. Mark Hyman (Zondervan 2013). Companion action plans are available for both books to facilitate group study.

I eat when I'm hungry, but I also eat sometimes when I'm bored, stressed, lonely, happy, 'hangry' or depressed. My thinking sometimes goes like this: *It's not autumn without my favorite sugary coffee drink next to me.* Or, *It's not summer without finger-licking barbeque chicken, potato salad, chips, and (of course) ice cream.* And let's not even talk about Christmas feasting. If food is meant to satisfy our physical hunger, why does it have to taste so good?

May God help us let go of the excessive food we eat, especially when what we *really* crave is His companionship. He's the God of *all* comfort, even our need to be comforted by food. We may be feeding the highs and lows of our emotions, but God is always there for us. When I put down my fork to pray or read His Word, He helps me refocus on what I *should* be doing. As I feast on the Bread of Life, He meets me where I am and helps me deal with my emotions in honest and constructive ways.

When ministering to the needs of others, especially the needs of our children, we often put ourselves last. We may feel like it's selfish to go to a weight-loss group or an exercise class. Yet our physical body is a treasure given by God, and maintaining our health shows we're grateful for it. Of course, time spent exercising and pursuing weight-loss goals needs to be in balance. Fitness can become an obsession for some women. So rather than spending long hours at the gym, consider playing outside with your kids. Go on a family bike ride. Play ball in the backyard. Take an evening walk with your husband. Hike with a friend. You'll love it! Create family memories relating to fitness and nutrition, and everyone around you will benefit.

Dress Smart

Dressing beautifully isn't a privilege reserved for the wealthy. It only requires some careful self-evaluation and knowledge of what compliments your unique figure, coloring, and shape. It's not how much you spend that matters but how knowledgeable you are in selecting what's right for you. Educate yourself by shopping in designer stores and trying on different styles to see how they look. Designer brands are cut to accommodate various body types, so find styles that are "you," and then invest in a few, or look for similar items in affordable stores. Quality is not unspiritual. A few outfits you love and feel great in are better than a closet full of clothes you don't like.

Have you ever noticed how an outfit that looks great on your friend may not be the best one for you? That's because we all have our own unique look. When you look at yourself in the mirror, what do you see, honestly? Are you tall, short, straight, curvy, or somewhere in between? If you don't like what the mirror's telling you, remember that God made you wonderfully (Ps. 139:14), and it's important to acquire an acceptance with the way He created you. Even if you aren't where you want to be physically, you can still make the most of who you are. With styles and stores for all shapes and sizes, women today can find clothing that flatters their own look.

When choosing garments and accessories such as purses, glasses, and jewelry, a fashion consultant would tell you to consider the following: your body type (curvy or straight), bone size, facial features, height, weight, and your overall look. Are your features soft or sharp? Is your general look straight or round? Longer jackets and skirts look better on tall women, and shorter jackets and skirts are more flattering on petite women. Consider how different weights of fabric look with your bone size and how the print of a fabric looks on you. No matter what shape or size you are, buying the correct clothing size will ensure that you look and feel more attractive and comfortable. If you're on a long-term weight loss track, be sure to wear clothes that fit you now. It's depressing to wear clothing that fits too baggy or too tight. Discount and secondhand stores are a great place to buy interim basics.

Beautiful Color

When selecting clothing, choose colors that bring life to your face and skin tone. The New York Times bestselling book, *Color Me Beautiful* by Carole Jackson made fashion history in 1973, when people suddenly began flocking to color consultants to be draped and color analyzed. The concept of discovering your own color palette for each season revolutionized the way we thought about fashion. For example, if a woman had a "summer" color palette and looked better in blues and purples, she didn't have to wear the traditional fall colors of oranges and browns. The book's basic concept was that each person belongs in one of the four basic seasons, or color groups, based on their hair and skin tone. One group of colors looks great on an individual, and the others don't (which is further evidence that God made us all uniquely). Check out the book if you're interested in learning more. Your color palette may be like your favorite colors as a child.

Hair, Skin, and Make-up

If you've ever experienced a bad haircut, you know what a difference a good one can make in your overall appearance. A woman's hair is her crowning glory, according to I Corinthians 11:15, so choose a style that compliments your line and facial features. And keep your hair clean and healthy!

Take good care of your skin as well. Remember Esther? Even though she was pick-her-out-of-the-crowd beautiful, she had to go through a year of beauty treatments before she was ready for the royal pageant. Most of us don't have the time or money to spend a year at the spa, but a little time, effort, and money is perfectly justifiable and can make a noticeable difference in how you look and feel about yourself.

A few cosmetics can also add to your beauty. I enjoy wearing make-up—in fact, I don't enjoy *not* wearing it. Get a good makeover occasionally to keep current on new colors and techniques.

Proverbs 31:30 tells us, "Charm is deceitful and beauty is passing, but a woman who fears the Lord, she shall be praised." A God-fearing woman has eternal beauty. Beauty is not the main place, but it does have a place. By taking care of her appearance, an attractive, well-kept woman shows kindness to those around her. Who would you rather spend time with—a person who cares about the way she looks or one who doesn't care at all?

Simply put, a husband is happy when his wife looks nice. If you're married, please your husband in this. It doesn't take a lot—even a few minutes a day can be enough. More importantly, please the Lord in this way. Do the best with what you've been given to be beautiful in your sphere of influence. The Proverbs 31 woman was dressed in lovely garments of linen and purple, but these were only an outward indication of her deep and lasting inner beauty.

For Discussion:

1. Why is external beauty important?

2. Think about a woman you know who is beautiful inside and out. How is she different than someone who is beautiful only on the outside?

3. List two righteous benefits of outward beauty:
   1)
   2)

For Prayer:

Pray to keep your perspective of beauty in balance—that you don't make it over important but you don't neglect it either.

For Homework and Application:

Go shopping!

Chapter Fifteen

Spiritual Make-up and Perfume

"His face shone like the sun." (Matthew 17:2)

Whether you wear make-up or not, there are a few essential items you won't want to do without. The first is what I call Radiance Foundation. In Exodus 34:29-35, Moses is described as having a glowing face after spending time in the Lord's presence. His face shone with such an obvious display of God's glory that he had to wear a veil because the children of Israel were afraid to look at him. The brightness of God's glory was simply too awesome for sinful people to see.

II Corinthians 3:7-18 explains that we who are in Christ have an even greater glory than Moses. Of course, it's not as obvious as it was with Moses, but have you ever noticed a certain glow about those who love the Lord? I've seen that glow on the faces of Christians around the country—church friends, prayer partners, and prison inmates. A person's background doesn't matter; Jesus can be seen in anyone who loves Him.

I Corinthians 3:18 says that Jesus has removed the veil, once and for all. After Jesus died, the veil in the temple was torn in two, and the way to God was no longer blocked by sin. Jesus, through His death, paid the penalty for sin, and now God is accessible to all who come to Him. Symbolically, Jesus removed the veil over our faces too.

Paul tells us in Galatians 3:24 that even though we couldn't keep the law, it was given as a tutor to bring us to God and show our need for a Savior. Some people still stumble over the law today, as if they're wearing a veil of confusion. They think they'll go to heaven because they are good people, or at least better than ax murderers. Since they keep *most* of the law, they think their goodness is a ticket to Paradise. But they're wrong.

Romans 3:23 says, "For all have sinned and fall short of the glory of God." Whether young or old, we're all sinners. But the good news of the gospel is that sinners are saved entirely by God's mercy through Jesus Christ.

The glory shining through us is God's righteousness, not ours. When we wear Radiance Foundation, the world sees a shining glory in our face—the mercy of our Father. Through the Holy Spirit, we grow in this glory as we keep looking to Jesus. Wouldn't it be great if others could see only Jesus in us—if they could see His love and mercy instead of our sins and blemishes?

Lipstick

The next essential beauty item is Praise Lipstick. Psalm 34:1 says, "I will extol the Lord at all times; his praise will always be on my lips" (NIV). Just like pretty shade of lipstick compliments any outfit, words of praise add beauty and color to our moments and days. Whenever we notice that praise isn't coming from our lips, we need to check out what *is* filling our hearts, as Matthew 12:34 reveals: "Out of the abundance of the heart, the mouth speaks."

What do we think about? What do we talk about? What consumes our time? Philippians 4:8 reminds us of this truth: "Finally, brethren, whatever things are true, whatever things are noble, whatever things are just, whatever things are pure, whatever things are lovely, whatever things are of good report, if there is any virtue and if there is anything praiseworthy—meditate on these things."

Perhaps it's time for a fresh application of Praise Lipstick. It's the only way to avoid the dangerous outcome in Psalm 140:3: "The poison of vipers is on their lips" (NIV). That's what happens to the person who applies the lipstick brand I call *Poison of Vipers*.

Imagine an attractive woman who's dressed in an elegant evening gown and is also wearing black lipstick. The black lipstick would not only distract from her pretty face, it would also wash out her natural coloring. This Poison of Vipers brand represents lips that speak unkindly about others. With self-promotion in mind, the woman who wears it is quick to make hateful comments and spread gossip. Her lipstick brand kills praise and honesty, and after a while, it kills faith. Just as black lipstick has its own popularity, so the Poison of Vipers brand has a faithful following. Don't let it kiss you. Keep praising the Lord!

Perfume

Next, douse yourself with the sweet-smelling Perfume of Knowing Christ. In the same way that fragrant perfume compliments your presentation, this spiritual quality is vital for your beauty. If you possess all the other qualities but forget this one, it's like a woman who dresses perfectly but smells bad. Her stinky odor ruins others' impression of her.

The main goal of our faith is to know Christ, and knowing Him is the result of the gospel. Christ is our security, our hope, our reason for joy, our lifelong pursuit, and our eternal home.

John 17:3 says, "And this is eternal life, that they may know You, the only true God, and Jesus Christ whom You have sent.*" Sometimes we make Christianity into a dead religion, but we must remember it's a relationship. Jesus reconciled us back to God, and that means He brought us back into relationship with Himself. In fact, all the qualities and garments we've studied so far are sustained by our relationship with Him.

Some people are attracted to the Fragrance of Knowing Christ in your life, and they desire it for themselves. Others don't like it because it smells like death to them. II Corinthians 2:14-16 describes Christ's fragrance this way:

"Now thanks be to God, who always leads us to triumph in Christ and through us diffuses the fragrance of His knowledge in every place. For we are to God the fragrance of Christ among those who are being saved and among those who are perishing. To the one we are the aroma of death leading to death, and to the other the aroma of life leading to life. And who is sufficient for these things?"

Wouldn't it be great if those near us were aware of Jesus' presence in us, in the same way they're aware of our perfume? Our testimony for Christ goes beyond the words we speak to include the fragrance we spread when we know Him. People in the world don't understand this. Christ's fragrance convicts them and causes them to realize their sin. They may not want you around when they sense God's presence through the relationship you have with Him. But take the risk anyway, and stir up some controversy by wearing the Perfume of Knowing Christ.

Another sweet perfume is the rich, aromatic Fragrance of Prayer. In Revelation 5:8 we read that the Lord enjoys our prayers as if they were perfumed incense. He remembers each petition and saves them all in golden bowls. In Bible times, women often let the aroma of incense soak into their clothes, like perfume, so they would smell of the fragrance. And because of the heat of that climate, the incense was probably a deodorant too. Although this prayer perfume is used only to please the Lord, people notice the effects when you wear it— it's the kind of scent that arrives before you do. And at times when you need to use a lot of it, the strength of the aroma will bring tears to your eyes. The Fragrance of Prayer is precious to the Lord. Prayer is a wonderful gift. However, it's not always easy, and sometimes it may seem like you're talking into the air. That's because prayer is hard on the flesh. When you finally take the time to do it, sometimes at that very moment you remember all the people you're supposed to call and all the things you're supposed to do. The enemy doesn't like it, and he may send distractions to keep you away from it. But to maintain a relationship with our Lord, communion with Him is necessary. He set it up this way so you'd come to Him often!

I Thessalonians 5:17 instructs us to "pray without ceasing." This can only be done if we're abiding with Him, step by step, with prayers like *Lord, please help me in my conversation with this person* or *Thank you for this sunshine* or *Lord, why am I feeling depressed?* or *Be with those people in the ambulance.* He also loves it when we share our deeper thoughts in prayer with Him, such as, w*hat do You mean by this passage of Scripture?* He answers those too—perhaps not right away, but you'll find that something will come up to bring an understanding, and you'll know it's His answer. He is sweet that way. A friendship doesn't go very far if the friends don't spend time talking to each other. In the same way, prayer is crucial in our relationship with God.

"How precious also are Your thoughts to me, O God! How great is the sum of them! If I should count them, they would be more in number than the sand; when I awake, I am still with You" (Psalm 139:17-18).

His thoughts toward us are more than we could ever know. Psalm 139:3 says that He's intimately acquainted with all our ways. He's more concerned for us than *we* are. Why wouldn't we want to talk with Him? He treasures the times we pray; they're like captivating incense to Him. The timeless beauty of prayer fragrance reaches heaven. Wear prayer!

For Discussion:

1. List three ways you can know God:
   1)
   2)
   3)

2. Why are nonbelievers uncomfortable around believers?

3. What's a good way to handle a situation where others are gossiping?

For Prayer

1. As you read Psalm 139, let the Lord minister His love to you. Pray that you will understand how special you are to Him.

2. Repent of any habits of gossip you have and ask God for help to change. Ask Him to help your mouth to learn new responses.

3. Pray for praise to be on your lips and in your heart this week.

For Homework and Application:

1. Read Mark 3: 1-5. In these verses, Jesus was angry.
   a) How did He not fight the battle?

   b) How did He have faith, offer praise, and wait for God to act?

   c) How did He do what was right?

2. By faith, become more aware of God's presence and His love for you.

3. Practice being more intentional with prayer.

Chapter Sixteen

Jewelry

"O you afflicted one, tossed with tempest, and not comforted, behold, I will lay your stones with colorful gems, and lay your foundations with sapphires. I will make your pinnacles of rubies, your gates of crystal, and all your walls of precious stones. All your children shall be taught by the Lord, and great shall be the peace of your children." (Isaiah 54:11-13)

Jewelry adds the finishing touch to an outfit that makes it complete. With the right accessories, a plain black dress becomes an evening gown. A sparkly necklace or brilliant earrings can brighten a person's face and make it appear more attractive. Jewelry not only adds beauty, it may also be a sign that someone loves you.

A few years ago, my husband bought me an exquisite stained-glass jewelry box and said he would fill it up in the years to come. Since then, he's gifted me with a special piece of jewelry on most every Christmas, anniversary, and birthday. I feel very loved. What a man!

Did you know the Lord has jewels for His bride too? Isaiah 54 is written to us, His bride, and in verses 11-12, He promises to surround us with beautiful jewels. Also, in Revelation 21:19, He promised jewels to His church in heaven. Even the foundation of heaven's golden city will be set in jewels, with seven layers composed of different precious stones. Imagine the splendor! We're impressed here on earth by tiny diamonds or rubies in a ring setting. Picture giant blocks of gems making up the city foundation—yet another sign of the amazing love God has for us. When we wear His spiritual jewelry, we show the world a glimpse of His glory.

First, be dazzled by the **Earrings of Submission**. Imagine these as diamond earrings. Diamonds are among the hardest substances known. Through intense pressure, they're formed and purified, and the more pressure they endure, the purer they become. Coal is created from dead plant life under the pressure of the earth or under water, and after many years, diamonds form from some of this coal. Take hope that God has a good purpose in the pressure we must endure in life.

As we submit ourselves to God, the process of dying to ourselves gets intense too, like the pressure of forming diamonds out of coal. Not only that, but this dying process often seems to continue in kind of a holding pattern.

Submitting becomes easier when we love the one we're submitting to. Exodus 21:5-6 describes the earring of submission and what happened if a bond slave didn't want to leave his master when it was time to be set free: "But if the servant plainly says, 'I love my master, my wife, and my children; I will not go out free;' then his master shall bring him to the judges. He shall also bring him to the door, or to the doorpost, and his master shall pierce his ear with an awl; and he shall serve him forever."

Out of our love for the Lord, we can decide to submit to Him as well, like the bond slave. Whenever we submit to God, we openly acknowledge that His way is better than ours. Submission is an act of humility.

James 4:6-7 says it this way: "God resists the proud, but gives grace to the humble. Therefore, submit to God." Submitting shows we trust Him. Remember that when you're facing difficult times and are tempted to go your own way. Submitting to God brings peace and protection. Realizing how good He is and how much He cares increases your love for Him.

In marriage, God gives us practice ground for submission. When we submit to our husbands, we promote peace. Sometimes it's frightening to trust the Lord in this, especially when we have different opinions about a situation. But a family with two ruling heads doesn't function well. When you're submitted to the Lord, it's easier to follow the leadership of your husband.

Learn to flex your will on issues that aren't significant in the long run. There is no perfect man, and your husband will make mistakes. Be there to offer your gentle opinions so you can make joint decisions, but when a final decision comes down to him, support him. God has given him the tools for the job, and he's usually right. Too many women talk and laugh about their husband behind his back. However, God wants you to support him from your heart, in deed and truth (I John 3:18).

God honored Sarah for her submission to her husband, Abraham (I Peter 3:6 and Heb. 11:11). Even though Abraham had a few blunder years, Sarah still submitted. And because her submission was based on her faith in God, she had no reason to fear. She knew God was big enough to cover both her *and* her husband.

When submission to God comes first, it also means you will not submit if your husband or anyone else asks you to do something that isn't honoring to God. Acts 5:1-11 illustrates this principle with the story of Ananias and Sapphira. This married couple was part of the vibrant early church, where believers shared all their belongings with each other. Like others in the fellowship, Ananias and Sapphira decided to sell some of their property and share the proceeds with the believers. it was a noble thing to do; however, they kept some of the money for themselves and then lied about it. When Ananias brought the proceeds to the apostles, Peter rebuked him and Ananias fell over dead. Sapphira arrived later, and God gave her the chance to be honest. Not knowing what had happened to her husband, Sapphira died too for lying to the Holy Spirit about the money. Submitting first to God can keep us from tragic mistakes.

Just as diamonds are one of the most valuable gems on earth, submission is one of the most valuable jewels we can wear for our audience in heaven. The Lord describes submission as *precious* (I Peter 3:3). Compliment your look with the precious diamond earrings of submission.

Next, let's look at the **Necklace of Discernment and Sound Judgment** found in Proverbs 3:21-22: "Keep sound wisdom and discretion, so they will be life to your soul and adornment to your neck" (NASB). The necklace of discernment is an important piece of jewelry. If you were to wear a choker necklace that fits snug around your neck, you'd always be aware of it. Picture the Necklace of Discernment and Sound Judgment as this kind of snug necklace.

Spiritually, discernment and sound judgment are essential to our Christian walk. Without them, we'd easily slip into the temptation and deception that surround us.

For those of us raising a family, we need a double dose of discernment and sound judgment to guide decisions like where to let our children go and with whom. These spiritual qualities also help protect our marriage from attack. And when circumstances spin out of control, they prompt us to pray.

Pray for discernment in these areas:

1. Spirituality: Test everything with Scripture, especially if something seems off. If you're not sure about a decision, pray about it and seek advice from someone you trust who knows God's Word. If you're married, ask your husband, even if he's not a believer (I Cor. 14:35).
2. Friendships: Be careful in friendships. People often have hidden agendas and may bring you down. Be selective about who you share your heart with.
3. Temptations: Use discernment in friendships with men. Beware of those who promise bliss. The enemy can disguise himself as an angel of light (II Cor. 11:14). Be careful what you think about, look at, and listen to. You know your areas of weaknesses so don't entertain them. Memorize Scripture to quote in times of temptation—that's how Jesus dealt with Satan in the wilderness. How much more we need God's Word!
4. Prayer: Ask God for help. He wants to give you discernment in prayer and show you who and what to pray for. Have you ever felt a burden for someone, only to find out later that they were going through a trial at the same time you felt the burden?
5. Family and friends: Exercise discernment for your children, your family, and your friends. As the body of Christ, we are responsible for each other If our foot was about to step off a cliff, wouldn't our eyes, legs, and brain try to stop us from falling? The radiant beauty of the Necklace of Discernment and Sound Judgment only magnifies its importance in our lives.

Next, Proverbs 1:9 describes the **Necklace and Garland of Obedience**: "They (God's words) are a garland to grace your head and a chain to adorn your neck" (NLT). Do you see the words of God as lovely? Think of a little flower girl in a wedding with a garland of flowers on her head. This precious child willingly follows her parents' instruction to "walk down the aisle like you're supposed to." It's good when a child regards her parent's instruction. And it's good when we take in God's words and obey them willingly.

The Word is perfect and good, like a round necklace, a complete circle that's adorned with one treasure after another. God's Word is also like a garland of flowers—new and fresh every day with unique and fragrant messages of comfort, healing, and encouragement.

Spend time enjoying God's Word each day, and you'll find yourself wanting to obey it more and more. The Lord is so good! Why do we sometimes miss that?

In Luke 15:20-22, when the father ran to greet his prodigal son, he gave his son a ring that symbolized complete acceptance and forgiveness. In our spiritual wardrobe, **The Ring of Relationship** is a unique piece. With all that our hands stay busy with each day, the ring is always there to remind us of our relationship with the Lord. It shows the world our commitment to Him. Everything we do and say is done with this meaningful ring on.

A wedding ring also symbolizes commitment—the commitment of marriage. For women who marry, life changes dramatically. They're no longer alone, they're known by a new name, and they share their possessions. With abandon, they gladly begin a new family unit with their husband.

Even greater changes occur when you begin a relationship with the Lord. Since you're a new creation, *everything* changes. Let others know you belong to someone special, to Jesus. Let them see how everything you are and everything you have belongs to Him. They will know you are His because of your life and testimony.

The Ring of Relationship symbolizes God's acceptance and unconditional love for you. The father of the prodigal was so full of love for his son that he didn't focus on how his son had hurt him, taken his money, and despised his home. The father forgave it all because he loved his son. The Lord has done the same for each one of us. We can wear the Ring of Relationship with confidence and thankfulness, extending the Lord's grace and love to others. In this way, we show that He has this ring for them too.

Be Careful How You Wear Your Ring

"As a ring of gold in a swine's snout, so is a lovely woman who lacks discretion," says Proverbs 11:22. Many things can turn your nose into a snout: distasteful jokes, cruel comments, or immodesty to name a few. Trust God to bring you the fun and joy you need, and don't seek it in impure ways.

When we degrade ourselves by being inconsiderate in our dress, words, or actions, people remember the negative image we project. It's hard to forget the times when women I know dress immodestly or act out of control. It's also hard to think of certain celebrities in any other way than their offensive performances. Discretion protects our spiritual beauty. Use discretion liberally—unless, of course, you like the swine-ish look.

Here She Is…

Did you know the Lord has placed a **Crown of Lovingkindness** on your head? According to Isaiah 51:11 and Psalm 103:4, He's crowned you with joy, lovingkindness, and tender mercies. We've been graced by God with this honor, and His love is our reason for joy and confidence. With this crown, He has placed His priceless love and compassion on us.

Wearing a jeweled crown out in public is an uncommon sight these days. It makes you stop and take notice, doesn't it? In the same way, others take notice whenever you let God's glory shine through your life, like wearing a shimmering crown on your head. So, walk tall, knowing you don't have to fear because His perfect love casts it all away. Allow the Lord's glory to shine through you—it's an honor!

For Discussion:

1. How can you develop spiritual discernment without judging or criticizing?

2. Write down one way you've submitted and obeyed the Lord.

3. How did you feel before and after submitting?

4. A fine clothing store once hung this slogan in the window: "Classic is Standing Out, Not Sticking Out."
   What's your definition of *indiscretion*?
   Give an example of a clothing choice and a conversation topic that show indiscretion.

   1) Clothing choice:
   2) Conversation topic:

For Prayer:

1. Pray for a submissive and obedient heart to the Lord.

2. Pray for spiritual discernment to recognize temptation for what it is.

3. Ask the Lord's to open your eyes to any habits of indiscretion you may have, and that He will show you ways to change.

For Homework:

Because we wear the Lord's Ring of Relationship, everything is different. List three ways *you* are different because of this relationship:
1)
2)
3)

Conclusion

After studying the many spiritual garments throughout this book, I hope you've gained a deeper awareness of God's love for you. As you grow in a living, daily relationship with Him, He will show you by His Spirit when to slip on that Apron of Kindness or those Pajamas of Compassion. He will shine His beauty through you, and as He gives you the character qualities you need, He'll help you share His love with your family, friends, and neighbors. This will happen as you "clothe yourselves with the Lord Jesus Christ" (Rom. 13:14 NIV).

Have *you* clothed yourself with Jesus? You can do this by simply believing in Him and asking Him to be Lord of your life. Have you ever done things you regret (like everyone else in the world)? Well, that's why Jesus came to save you. He took the punishment for your sin by dying on the cross. He rose from the dead and wants to live in your heart. He wants to cover you and make you righteous—in right standing before God. This is the gospel, the good news from the Bible. If you are already a believer, it's important to continually realize your need to trust Him and to be clothed in *His* righteousness, as it says in Galatians 3:27: "For all of you who were baptized into Christ have clothed yourselves with Christ" (NIV).

Acts 4:13 tells us that people recognized something different about the disciples when they had spent time with Jesus. We'll be recognized that way, too, when we're clothed in Him. Just as people notice what we're wearing, I pray the Lord will be evident and noticed in us by what we do. Do we spend our lives operating in the deeds of the flesh—in envy, greed, competition, or immorality? Or do we love others the way Jesus does, through acts of kindness, forgiveness, and humility? One way to find out if we're truly clothed with Jesus is to do a fruit inspection. We can ask ourselves: *Is God's love the produce of my life?*

Colossians 3:14 says, "But above all these things put on love, which is the bond of perfection." Love is the most wonderful attribute of all, and it encompasses all others. It is the main goal of our lives, as the Apostle Paul says in I Timothy 1:5: "Now the purpose of the commandment is love from a pure heart, from a good conscience, and from sincere faith."

Physical beauty is a fleeting pursuit. But when we arise and shine in the Lord's love, we have true beauty and others see it. I Timothy 2:9-10 speaks of how a woman should dress—appropriately, modestly, with good deeds, and not overly concerned with outward beauty. The most attractive people are those who reflect their beautiful Lord.

Inward beauty doesn't end with this life. The book of Revelation describes the saints in heaven as clothed in white robes, which represent the Lord's complete covering for our sins. We'll wear these most incredibly pure garments there, purified by the blood of the only Son of God, Jesus.

Heaven will be a glorious place. Here's a sneak preview from Revelation 7:15-17:

"Therefore, they are before the throne of God, and serve Him day and night in His temple. And He who sits on the throne will dwell among them. They shall neither hunger anymore nor thirst anymore; the sun shall not strike them, nor any heat; for the Lamb who is in the midst of the throne will shepherd them and lead them to living fountains of waters. And God will wipe away every tear from their eyes."

Heaven—I can't wait! All our trials and heartaches will be over. We'll see our loved ones who have gone to be with the Lord, we won't have to deal with the sinful flesh and its weakness, and we we'll have new bodies. Hallelujah! The New Jerusalem will be made entirely out of precious stones, with streets of pure gold, and gates of giant pearls. The best part of all will be seeing Jesus face to face and experiencing His love together. We will live forever, worshipping our wonderful Lord.

May God be with you as you continue in His love, sharing Him with others and living out The Wardrobe of Inner Beauty.

The Wardrobe of Inner Beauty Fashion Show

After your group has completed this Bible study, you can celebrate together and see all the garments modeled. Instructions follow for putting on your own 'Inner Beauty Fashion Show' and luncheon.

Background and Instructions

Several years ago, after months of discouragement in my life, the Lord brought freedom and healing to me through Isaiah 60:1-2. By meditating on this scripture, I found purpose again, and that purpose was to shine Jesus' love to the hurting world around me. It's my prayer that other women will experience the joy and freedom I've found in discovering my own spiritual wardrobe.

This fashion show has been presented at churches, retreats, and Bible studies. Besides being a lot of fun, it's opened women's eyes to seeing spiritual qualities in a new and practical light. To plan your own fashion show, begin by choosing a commentator, five or six women models, and one pre-teen girl model. At least one of your adult models should be able to ham it up a bit. Give this one the nose ring and pig mask, the black lipstick, the Garment of Humility, and the Garment of Power. Give the preteen model the Shoes of Forgiveness and the Garland of Obedience.

Prepare a room for your show by setting up tables facing the front, with an aisle down the center. Mark the floor with a few masking-tape X's for models to walk to, pose, and turn around. Create a light, fun atmosphere with upbeat instrumental background music. Decorate tables with flowers, teacups, or costume jewelry.

Most of the suggested clothing and accessories should be easy to find among the models. Someone is sure to still have (and fit in) their wedding dress. Someone may have diamond or fake diamond earrings. Cheap dark lipstick can be purchased at a discount store. A garland can be strung with flowers from someone's yard. If you can't find everything, be resourceful. For example, we made a pig mask out of construction paper and put a ring of yellow yarn through the nose. For subsequent shows, I found a pig snout at a party store, which worked great.

May the Lord bless you with a fun and encouraging 'Inner Beauty Fashion Show'! Please write me a note or email—I'd love to hear how your show turns out.

Or if you would like me to come and help you with your event, I would love to! Please contact me. This study can be presented as a refreshing and creative women's retreat as well.

Bonnie Foxley
PO Box 933
Woodinville, WA 98072
Or email: **bbfoxley@gmail.com**

The Wardrobe of Inner Beauty Fashion Show

Introduction

Commentator:

Do you ever wake up in the morning and feel like you have nothing to wear? Perhaps you can't find one thing in your closet that matches your mood or activity that day. Well then, I have good news! The Lord has given you an incredible wardrobe, with the perfect outfit for every day you'll ever face.

Isaiah 60:1-2 says, "Arise, shine; for your light has come! And the glory of the Lord is risen upon you. For behold, the darkness shall cover the earth, and deep darkness the people; but the Lord will arise over you, and His glory will be seen upon you." As Christian women, we have something beautiful to shine out to a spiritually dark world, and that is Jesus, who is God's glory. Let's get rid of whatever holds us back so that we too can "arise and shine."

Throughout Scripture, the Lord tells us to put on certain spiritual qualities, just as we would put on articles of clothing and jewelry. If we were to view these spiritual qualities as modern-day fashions, what would they look like? In today's show, we'll explore some possibilities. Look at these spiritual fashions, and find out how living for Jesus can make you a truly beautiful woman.

Garment of Salvation

We begin with one of the most special pieces of clothing in our show—the Garment of Salvation. What could be lovelier than this pure white wedding dress modeled by (model's name)? As Christians, we look forward to the marriage feast of the Lamb, which is coming soon.

Matthew 22:12 says that wedding garments will be required for admission to this party of all parties. However, the Garment of Salvation cannot be bought in any store. It can't be earned by good works or inherited through the family line. Instead, God purchased this garment at a very high cost for everyone who will receive it. The price was His Son, Jesus, who willingly gave His life and took the punishment for all our sins. When He clothes us with the Garment of Salvation, He washes us clean and pure, like a white wedding dress. Thank you, (model's name).

The Garment of Praise

From the storehouse of Isaiah 61:3, we find the next item of clothing, the Garment of Praise. This piece is represented by a sparkling sequin gown modeled by (model's name). The Garment of Praise replaces a spirit of heaviness, which is what we *used* to wear. How freeing it is to realize we don't have to be burdened down with the weight of sin and depression! Instead, we can live each day with a heart of thankfulness and praise to Him. When we're clothed with the Garment of Praise, the world around us can't help but notice our spiritual glow. Thank you for modeling the Garment of Praise for us, (model's name).

The Robe of Righteousness

The Robe of Righteousness from Isaiah 61:10 is modeled by (model's name). This garment is represented by a white fur coat.

The word *sacrifice* comes to mind when I think of a fur coat because of all the little animals that had to die to purchase it. And yet, Jesus' sacrifice for us was even more costly than this. John 3:16 says He gave it all for our sake, and 2 Corinthians 5:21 explains why when it says, "He made Him who knew no sin to be sin for us, that we might become the righteousness of God in Him."

Fur coats aren't popular with animal activists. Similarly, neither is righteousness popular in the eyes of the world. But far better than the world's acclaim is the Bible's promise to us in Revelation 7:9,13-14, that we who are clothed spiritually with the Lord's righteousness will be clothed with a pure white robe of righteousness in eternity, where we'll be with our wonderful Lord and Savior, Jesus. Thank you, (model's name).

Garment of Compassion

The storehouse of Colossians 3:12 provides us with a whole wardrobe of practical, everyday pieces. Here is the Garment of Compassion, represented by smooth pajamas, a soft robe, and fuzzy slippers.

This pajama ensemble might be worn when taking care of a baby or a young child in the middle of the night. Whether it's a 2 a.m. feeding, a nightmare, or teething pain, being cradled in Mommy's arms in the rocking chair is what's needed. A mother's tender compassion helps soothe the pains and fears of a child so he or she can return to a peaceful sleep.

The spiritual Garment of Compassion does the same for those around us. A soft, reassuring word or a gentle touch feels so comforting to a soul in need. Thank you, (model's name).

Garment of Kindness

Next, we have the Garment of Kindness. Clothing that represents kindness may come in many styles, colors, and textures. Here we see it as an apron, modeled by (model's name).

This cute number can be worn when baking a treat for your family, such as a favorite pie or cake for no special reason. It can be worn to whip up a batch of cookies to surprise a neighbor who needs encouragement. Or you can wear it while making dinner for a new mom, someone who's ill, or a friend in financial need.

As you can see, the Garment of Kindness is very practical, with the potential to bless many people in our lives. Thank you, (model's name).

Garment of Humility

We're told twice in Scripture to be clothed with humility—in Colossians 3:12 and I Peter 5:5. So the Garment of Humility must be a crucial article of clothing. This garment is represented by plain work clothes, like these sweats and jeans modeled by (model's name).

There's certainly nothing flashy about this humble outfit, nothing to draw our attention at all. But the woman who wears it is ready to get in there and do whatever needs to be done. Notice that (model's name) has her hair pulled back and a sponge in hand so she can scrub those stubborn, hard-to-clean areas. In the process, she may rub up against some grimy stuff, like ovens and toilets. Spiritually, *we* rub up against grimy stuff too—perhaps offensive jokes or profanities we don't want to hear. But we can be washed clean from *all* of this by the healing, refreshing water of God's Word.

Humility can be scary. We may be afraid we'll go unnoticed or be taken advantage of. But when we ponder the humility of Jesus, shown by the way He took on the form of a bondservant, we realize that this is, indeed, a most precious garment (Phil 2:6-8). You are in God's hands, and He sees every deed done in humility and love. He remembers them all and will reward you in His time (I Peter 5:5). Thank you, (model's name).

Garment of Gentleness

Next, for the Garment of Gentleness, (model's name) wears an angora sweater. Notice how soft the sweater looks and feels to the touch, never scratchy or irritating. On the inside it's gentle next to the skin, and on the outside, it feels soothing and comforting to anyone who comes in contact with it.

See how the sweater's material also softens (model's name)'s face? Gentleness is contagious. Watching someone practice gentleness is so appealing that it diffuses the atmosphere of any environment. Proverbs 15:1 says, "A soft answer turns away wrath." Gentleness softens harshness, and it's the opposite of contention. Wearing the Garment of Gentleness is vital for beauty of speech, behavior, and attitude. Thank you, (model's name).

Garment of Patience

The Garment of Patience is the last article modeled today from the Colossians 3:12 storehouse. Perhaps you're thinking, *what a difficult garment to possess!* You're right. In the flesh, this garment is impossible to wear, but, the Master Designer Himself, the Holy Spirit, has custom made this piece just for you. It's from His Fruit of the Spirit Collection.

Here we see an intricate, hand-knit sweater worn by (model's name). Many long hours of work went into creating this lovely item to keep its wearer warm year after year through the cold winters. Wearing the Garment of Patience warms you, too, whenever unexpected, icy words blast your way. The warmth continues, even when snow flurries and turbulent blizzards of trials blow through your life.

According to James 1:4, wearing the Garment of Patience will make you complete in all things, and I Peter 2:20 adds that you will also find favor with God.

Lord, please knit patient sweaters for us today—right now! Thank you, (model's name).

Garment of Joy

Look at the bright and cheerful colors in this Garment of Joy worn by (model's name). In Psalm 30:11, David describes this garment as the new fashion replacing the drab, outdated sackcloth tunic. What a delightful change, wouldn't you say?

The interesting thing about the Garment of Joy is that we can't put it on ourselves. Only the Lord can dress us in this piece. In today's fashion industry, we see many fleeting pleasure garments, but they all wear out quickly. Accept no substitutes for this sought-after item!

The *true* Garment of Joy gives us strength, lifts our countenance, and blesses everyone around us. Thank you, (model's name).

The Garment of Power

In Luke 24:49, Jesus told His disciples to wait in Jerusalem until they were clothed in power. The power Jesus spoke of was, of course, the Holy Spirit. Practically, we can think of the Garment of Power as a workout suit, worn today by (model's name). (Model should flex her muscles to show off her strength.)

With the Holy Spirit, we have power to overcome sin, to love unlovable people, and to change the world for Jesus. As we do these things, we exercise all the spiritual characteristics we've learned. This is an outfit the Lord endows us with. So, wait on the Him to give you your workout gear and tennis shoes—and then go for it! Thank you, (model's name).

Shoes of Forgiveness

After we're saved, we're bathed—in a spiritual sense. In other words, our feet get dirty with worries, cares, and sin as we travel life's path. Just as Jesus washed His disciples' feet in John 13:3-17, we too should wash each other's feet. See these clear (or white) sandals modeled by (girl model's name)? Her feet are clean. Even though she made fun of her brother today, he forgave her. And she forgave him for using her toy without asking.

Let's walk in forgiveness toward each other. We all need it! When we forgive, we help clean the dirty spots off one another's feet as we journey together. Thank you, (model's name).

(If the Shoes of Forgiveness model is an adult, can substitute "husband" or "friend" for "brother" and "the harsh words he spoke to her" for "using her toy.")

The Garment of Strength and Dignity

The virtuous woman in Proverbs 31 is "clothed in strength and dignity." This stunning business suit, worn by (model's name), makes a statement of confidence, security, and self-control.

Without being domineering or pushy, the woman dressed in the Garment of Strength and Dignity handles affairs at home and in the world with solid trust in the Lord. *He* is her confidence.

She has no reason to fear. She's not ensnared by the fear of man or enemy but rests secure in God's love. She knows that whatever He has for her to do, He will provide all she needs to accomplish it. Thank you, (model's name).

Fine Linen and Purple

The Proverbs 31 woman is also clothed in Fine Linen and Purple, represented by this purple (and/or linen dress) worn by (model's name). This proverb doesn't imply that a woman must necessarily wear this color and fabric. Rather, at the time it was written in the Bible era, fine linen and purple represented the most expensive clothing available. Purple symbolized royalty.

The Proverbs 31 woman took good care of her family and her household, but she didn't stop there. She took good care of herself too. God doesn't want us to max out our credit card to obey this scripture, but He does want us to do the best we can with what we have.

Through the years, some Christians have said that beauty and fashion are vain and unspiritual. Perhaps spiritual pride, fear, or laziness have given them an excuse to let themselves go. But God created beauty to be enjoyed. And as we see with this stylish outfit, a nice piece of clothing can accentuate spiritual beauty as well.

I Peter 3:3-4 says, "Do not let your adornment be *merely* outward—arranging the hair, wearing gold, or putting on fine apparel--rather let it be the hidden person of the heart, with the incorruptible beauty of a gentle and quiet spirit, which is very precious in the sight of God."

Always remember that true beauty comes from within, from Jesus living inside of you. But don't forget the outside! Your husband and friends will be grateful. Thank you, (model's name).

Spiritual Make-up

(Model's name) models our spiritual makeup today.

First, (model's name) is wearing Radiance Foundation. Remember how Moses' face glowed after he'd been in the Lord's presence? Radiance Foundation reminds us of that glow, and it's described in II Corinthians 3:7-18. This scripture says that we who have the Holy Spirit have an even greater glory than Moses, and Christ Jesus has removed the veil, once and for all. Wouldn't it be great if everyone who saw our faces could see Jesus? Instead of noticing our blemishes, what if they only saw the mercy of our Father through His Son? *Lord, let others see Jesus in us!*

Also, notice (model's name)'s bright and shiny Praise Lipstick. It lights up her face, doesn't it? In Psalm 34:1 the Psalmist says he desires to have praise on his lips always. What better picture for praise than lipstick—an attractive addition to any ensemble. Spoken words of praise that reflect the color of the moment are the perfect complement to a woman of godly character. Thank you, (model's name).

Poison of Vipers Lipstick

(Model's name) now wears the Poison of Vipers Lipstick brand, as described in Psalm 140:3, which says. "The poison of vipers is on their lips" (NIV) This make-up item is certainly not advised for daily use. Notice how the dark purple-black color distracts from the beauty of (model's name)'s face? This lipstick washes out her natural coloring.

The woman who wears Poison of Vipers Lipstick represents someone who speaks unkindly and gossips about others. She is quick to make hurtful comments and spread shady opinions to boost her own ego. Her mouth is poisonous because it kills praise and honesty, and after a while, it kills faith.

Models wearing the Poison of Vipers line appear on the covers of top fashion magazines, enjoying the passing fame of this world. But don't let the venom of this deadly lipstick kiss you! Instead, keep praising the Lord. Thank you, (model's name).

The Perfume of Knowing Christ

The next two items modeled today require your sense of smell. First, the Perfume of Knowing Christ represents the lovely fragrance of those who have the knowledge of Him. This scent is spoken of in II Corinthians 2:14, where it says that through us, Jesus "diffuses the knowledge of His presence in every place." Just as perfume compliments (model's name)'s presentation, the spiritual quality of knowing Him completes your spiritual beauty. If you possess all the other qualities but forget this one, it's like a woman who dresses perfectly but smells badly. Her foul odor ruins the impression she makes, doesn't it?

The Perfume of Knowing Christ is the reason for our joy. He is our life-long pursuit and eternal home. Some people are attracted to this fragrance and want it for themselves. To others, the Fragrance of Knowing Christ smells like death, and they don't like it at all. But remember not to take their rejection personally because the same thing happened to Jesus Himself. Thank you, (model's name).

The Fragrance of Prayer

Another perfume to enjoy today is the rich, aromatic Fragrance of Prayer. In Revelation 5:8, we read that the Lord considers our prayers as sweet as perfumed incense. He saves them all in golden bowls and remembers each one. Women in Bible times often let the aroma of incense soak into their clothes as a perfume, and they also used it as a room deodorizer.

The Fragrance of Prayer perfume is only worn to please the Lord. It isn't something we show off to our brothers and sisters. In fact, when we need to use a lot of it, the strength of the aroma will bring tears to our eyes. The Fragrance of Prayer is very precious to the Lord. Thank you, (model's name).

Earrings of Submission

Now we move on to our jewelry collection. (Model's name) models some diamond earrings, which represent submission to God. I love how earrings make a person's eyes sparkle and bring extra brightness to the face. Besides their brilliance, diamonds are also one of the hardest substances on earth. They can endure much pressure, and the more pressure they endure, the purer they become.

An earring is a symbol of submission in Exodus 21:5-6, where it describes the bond slave who willingly stayed with his master because he loved him. As a symbol of this commitment, the master pierced his slave's ear.

Like bond slaves submitted to their master, we also decide to submit to our Lord out of love for Him. If we're married, we decide to submit to our husband as well. It may seem frightening to trust the Lord in this, especially when we have different views than our husband. Still, the Lord views loving submission as a good thing. So, remember to wear your earrings! Thank you, (model's name).

Necklace of Discernment

The Necklace of Discernment and Sound Judgment is another stunning piece of jewelry. Proverbs 3:21-22 reminds us to "keep sound wisdom and discretion, so they will be life to your soul and adornment to your neck" (NASB). See how this choker fits snugly around (model's name)'s neck? She's constantly aware of it.

Discernment and sound judgment are crucial spiritual qualities to pray for. Without them, we can easily slip and be deceived by the temptations all around us.

As wives and mothers, we need a double dose of discernment and sound judgment. These qualities will guide us as we make decisions about our children, such as where we allow them to go and with whom. They'll also help protect our marriage from attack. And when circumstances are out of our control, they will prompt us to pray. Thank you, (model's name).

Necklace and Garland of Obedience

Do we consider the words of God as lovely? Proverbs 1:9 says that His words are like a graceful wreath on the head and like ornaments about the neck. This garland and necklace look so pretty on (girl model's name). It's good when a child regards her parents' instruction. And it's good when *we* regard God's instruction from His Word—when we treasure and obey it.

God's Word is perfect. It's like a round necklace, a complete circle with one priceless treasure after another. It's also like a garland of flowers, new and fresh every day, with fragrant words of comfort, healing, and encouragement. Thank you, (model's name).

Ring of Relationship

When the father greeted his prodigal son in Luke 15:22, he gave him a ring, which symbolized complete acceptance and forgiveness. The Ring of Relationship is a meaningful piece of spiritual jewelry, represented by this gorgeous ring worn by (model's name), With all that our hands must do, the ring is always right there to remind us of our relationship with the Lord, and to show the world our commitment to Him. Every act is done with this ring on.

A wedding ring is also a symbol of commitment and relationship to our husband. Let's wear a Ring of Relationship—in a spiritual sense—to the Lord, to our children, to our family, and to our friends. Let's always accept, forgive, and love them unconditionally. Thank you, (model's name).

Nose Ring of Indiscretion

However, be careful how you wear your ring! Here, (model's name) wears the latest trend in nose rings. Proverbs 11:22 says, "As a ring of gold in a swine's snout, so is a lovely woman who lacks discretion." Many things can turn your nose into a snout: distasteful jokes, cruel comments, and immodesty to name a few. Discretion protects your spiritual beauty. Use it liberally—unless, of course, you like the swine-ish look. Thank you, (model's name).

Crown of Lovingkindness

Did you know that the Lord has put a jeweled crown on your head? According to Isaiah 51:11 and Psalm 103:4, He has crowned you with joy, lovingkindness, and tender mercies. God has placed His love and compassion on each one of us, like a crown, and *He* is the reason we have joy and confidence.

We can walk tall, knowing we have nothing to fear because His perfect love has cast it all away. And just as seeing a glittering tiara on someone's head makes us stop and take notice, His glory shining through our lives has the same effect, drawing others to Him. What an honor to be humble vessels of His glory!

Clothe Yourself with the Lord Jesus

We've seen a lot of beautiful fashions modeled today. Thinking about the important spiritual garments we've described, you may be wondering, how can I wear them all?

The answer is to clothe yourself with the Lord Jesus. Through His Spirit, He will tell you when to slip on that Apron of Kindness or those Pajamas of Compassion. He will cover you with *Himself,* and your life will shine with His beauty.

"For *all* of you who were baptized into Christ have clothed yourselves with Christ" (Galatians 3:27 NIV).

(Close in prayer.)

Clothing and Accessories for Fashion Show

Print this list with model's name beside each item and hang it in the models' dressing room:

1. Garment of Salvation - White wedding gown
2. Garment of Praise - Sequin gown
3. Robe of Righteousness - White fur coat
4. Garment of Compassion - Smooth pajamas, soft robe, and furry slippers
5. Garment of Kindness - Cute apron, mixing bowl, and wooden spoon
6. Garment of Humility - Sweat shorts, jeans, ponytail holder or headband, sponge, cleaning spray bottle, and bucket)
7. Garment of Gentleness - Angora sweater (Model can extend her arm as she walks down the aisle to let the audience touch fabric of her sleeve.)
8. Garment of Patience - Hand-knit sweater
9. Garment of Joy - Bright floral print dress
10. Garment of Power - Workout clothes or sweat suit (Model can flex her muscles, do jumping jacks, and/or lift a dumbbell as she walks down the aisle.)
11. Garment of Strength and Dignity - Business suit
12. Garment of Fine Linen and Purple - Linen dress or pant suit
13. Shoes of Forgiveness - Clear or white sandals
14. Spiritual Makeup - Make-up tastefully done, with foundation and lipstick featured
15. Poison of Vipers Lipstick - Dark purple or black lipstick (Model should move through audience pretending to whisper and gossip, perhaps pointing a finger and sneering or shaking her head.)
16. The Perfume of Knowing Him - Sweet floral perfume

(Model can spray a little perfume on a scarf and hold it out for audience to smell if they want to. However, be aware of fragrance-sensitive members and don't overdo it.)

17. Fragrance of Prayer - Rich, strong perfume (same instructions as #16)
18. Earrings of Submission - Diamond stud earrings or fake diamond earrings
19. Necklace of Discernment - Choker or tight-fitting necklace
20. The Garland and Necklace of Obedience - Fresh flower garland and long bead necklace
21. Nose Ring of Indiscretion - Gold hoop earring in a pig mask or pig nose
    (Model should dress tacky and immodestly, swaying around. Suggest a short dress with bra showing and fake tattoos.)
22. Ring of Relationship - Wedding ring
23. Crown of Lovingkindness - Crown or tiara

About the Author

Bonnie Foxley is passionate about sharing the good news of Jesus Christ in a multitude of creative ways. Music has been the primary outlet, with her husband, as they have written songs, recorded CDs and performed throughout the Western states. She loves to encourage women to live more fully in the Lord and in their true beauty of His grace. She is a women's Bible teacher and worship leader. She studied the Bible through Calvary Chapel Bible College. Bonnie lives in Woodinville, WA with her husband of 34 years, Bryan. They have three grown children and five grandsons. Follow Bonnie on her blog: www.bbfoxley.wordpress.com

71927829R00089

Made in the USA
San Bernardino, CA
21 March 2018